D1714022

Lynn Hall's Dog Stories

Other Books by the Author

Gently Touch the Milkweed
A Horse Called Dragon
Ride a Wild Dream
The Secret of Stonehouse
The Shy Ones
Sticks and Stones
Too Near the Sun

Lynn Hall's
Dog Stories

ILLUSTRATED BY JOSEPH CELLINI

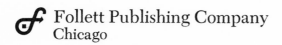

Follett Publishing Company
Chicago

ISBN 0-695-40321-4 Titan binding
ISBN 0-695-80321-2 Trade binding

Library of Congress Catalog Card Number:
76-184457

First Printing

for Carol

Stories

Someday

The sun had been up for only a short time, but already the grass was dried and the oppressive heat of an Iowa summer day was more reality than promise. In the backyard of the Methodist parsonage, the open cellar doors were stained sunrise pink.

I didn't notice the morning, though, as I came up into it from the dark cellar. My eyes, which usually had a nearsighted squint, were wide and unseeing with wonder.

I was ten, but small for my age. My handed-down chenille bathrobe trailed in the grass. It flapped open at every step, exposing my horsehead-printed pajamas tucked into the tops of my cowboy boots.

As I crossed the backyard of the parsonage toward my own yard across the alley, my mind was still full of the miracle in the cellar. I barely noticed the Boston terrier from up the street, and he was one of my best friends.

Into the house I floated, heedlessly stiff-arming the screen door and letting it slam behind me. I was not a door slammer by nature. Mother glanced away from the tent-shaped toaster, opened her mouth to reprove me for the slam, then decided not to.

Deftly lowering the side walls of the toaster just before the bread began to burn, she asked, "Well, did they get born all right?"

"It was the most wonderful thing I ever saw in my whole life," I said in a high soft voice. "Thank you for letting me."

I sat down in front of the glass of orange juice, drained it, then went on in a voice more nearly normal.

"I didn't know they—came out—like that. Every time a puppy came out I cried, but it wasn't because I was sad or anything. Just because I was so excited. And Daisy didn't care a bit if I was there. She liked having me there. The puppies were in a kind of sack and Daisy took it off of them so they could breath and—"

"That's fine, honey, but I don't think we want to hear all those details at the breakfast table."

The minister's wife was a close family friend, and by prearrangement at my begging request, had called in the middle of the night to say that Daisy's pups were about to be born and if anyone wanted to watch he'd better come a-running. I had gone galloping across the dark backyards, had sat for three hours on an upturned coal bucket in the basement, had stroked the head of the homely little brindled dog between deliveries, had fought down my queasiness at the sight and smell of the birth, and had, for those few hours, held hands with God.

The rest of the family came in and knocked away the last of the holy mood—my father in his blue uniform that smelled of fuel oil; Jan, who was thirteen, beautiful, and omniscient; and Lois, who at five was already a more good-natured daughter than I could ever hope to be.

Jan asked, "Did you really get up in the middle of the night just to see that dog have her puppies? You sure are crazy."

With this encouragement I repeated the account of the births, stopping just short of forbidden goriness.

Father said wearily, "Now I suppose she's got to have a puppy."

I glanced at Mother, my eyes wide with apprehension. I had been led to believe that the permission was secured. If Daddy said no now...

Mother said, "I told Lynn she could have one of these puppies IF she does all the work and the housebreaking and IF they aren't all spoken for. After all, Daisy's a sweet little dog, and short-haired, and I imagine at least some of the puppies will take after her."

My father sighed and acquiesced, but not without a final grumble. "You know what happens every time they bring a dog home. It wets all over the house, and just when they get attached to it, it gets run over or poisoned or something, and everybody bawls."

I got up and began easing toward the back door.

"No you don't." Mother cut me off. "The puppies will still be there this afternoon. You trot upstairs and take a nap."

That afternoon I resumed my seat on the coal bucket in the parsonage basement. The puppies were dry now, and nursing. With my parents' permission secured and this wealth of puppies from which to choose, I felt strung up with joy. I was studying the seven pups when the minister's wife came down the stairs from the house.

"Before you decide which one you want," she said, "I'd better tell you that all but two have been spoken for. The only ones left are that brindled one in the middle and the little black runt. You can't see him now. I guess he's on the bottom of the heap there somewhere."

With the field thus narrowed the choice was simple. I fished the tiny black puppy up from the bottom and held him reverently, close to my face. His mouse-sized claws swam against my hand, and the already-dried umbilical cord scratched my palm. I shivered and cupped my hands lovingly around him.

In a psuedoprofessional way I turned him over and ascertained that he was indeed a he. Experience had taught me that boy puppies gained my mother's good will more easily than girl puppies. I wasn't sure why, but I suspected that it had something to do with the fact that my parents kept getting daughters.

Laying the pup against my chest, I said, "I want this one. Did you pick out names for them yet?"

The minister's wife knelt beside the box. Daisy's tail struck the bedding. "Yes, we named them all after flowers. Because of Daisy. That one you've got is Bachelor Buttons. Let's see if I can remember the others—Marigold, Rosebud, Jack-in-the-Pulpit, Dandelion, what was that other one..."

But I heard nothing after Bachelor Buttons. Buttons. My dog. The others held no further interest. I stayed in the basement as long as I could, gave Buttons a long good-night cuddle, and went home reluctantly.

All through supper I talked about Buttons. No one listened, but I couldn't seem to stop. I was still on the subject when supper was over and I stood beside Jan, drying the dishes. Jan was preoccupied with things more important than newborn pups, but for once she was kind enough not to say "Shut up and wipe the dishes. You're getting on my nerves."

"I'm going to teach him to do opposite commands," I said, just as though someone were listening. "You know, to lie down when you say 'Up' or to dance on his hind legs when you say 'Play dead.' It isn't any harder to train a dog to do opposite commands than—"

The phone rang. It was the minister's wife, talking to Mother. They were good friends and often called one another after supper, so I paid little attention until I heard "Yes, I'll tell her. No, I don't think so, just so she gets one of them. You'll be sure to save the other one for her, though? Jack-in-the-Pulpit? Well, that's appropriate." She laughed. "Listen, is our circle supposed to be in charge of the refreshments for Meyers' wedding, or..."

Bachelor Buttons was dead. I hardened my jaw and refused to cry in front of Jan. That's what I get for wanting the runt of the litter, I told myself bitterly. But there's still the other puppy. Ugly brindle color though, and an ugly name. Jack-in-the-pulpit... I dried a handful of silverware and dealt them into their partitioned drawer—knife, knife, fork, knife, spoon, spoon, fork. Jack-in-the-Pulpit.

The requisite six weeks could not have gone more slowly if they had been the last weeks of the school year. It was midsummer, and except for my regular chores of burning trash, cleaning my room, doing dishes, and mowing the lawn, my time was my own. Most of it was spent in the parsonage cellar.

The little brindle sausage was the first of the pups to show a slit of gleaming black eyeball. I knew it was because he was in a hurry to see me, and it was all the proof I needed that Jack was the pick of the litter. By now the black puppy was all but forgotten.

At last the six weeks were up and Jack and I entered the nerve-strung weeks of housebreaking. Because the cries of a lonesome puppy might annoy the neighbors, I was instructed to keep the pup indoors at night. I was more than willing because I could hardly bear to be out of sight of Jack, but the nights were nearly sleepless. Fear kept me awake, fear of waking to find a puddle or worse on the bedroom rug, fear of the every-threatening parental edict, "We just can't have this mess in the house, Lynn. You'll have to get rid of him."

Four or five times a night I got up, trembling in haste, pulled on my cowboy boots and bathrobe, and snatched up Jack, who was bumbling and sniffing around. Down the stairs we went on booted tiptoes, out the side door and into the safety zone of the black-green grass. I sat on the concrete steps and watched for action with eyes still reluctant to open and focus. Then, back in bed with the puppy safely drained, I was too roused by the night air to go to sleep.

Sometimes my inner warning system failed to wake me at the sound of Jack moving around, and in my dream I would hear an amplified torrent of rushing water. I'd wake, heart hammering. The light of the reading lamp would show the puddle and Jack, head low, tail wagging tentatively between his hocks.

Fortunately there was an upstairs bathroom and my folks' bedroom was downstairs, so I was able to mop things up undetected, unless the accident happened on the rug. Then there was no way to dry the spot, or to hide it, before morning.

Although I tried hard not to show it, the post-accident tension I felt was impossible to hide. I felt the pup's guilt as heavily as my own during the period a year or two before, when I had hoarded all my church offering money in hopes of buying a pony with it. Each morning I waited for Mother to go up to my room, see the damp place on the rug, and say, "Well, this is it. We can't put up with this mess any longer, Lynn. He'll have to go."

But the words were never spoken, and gradually the accidents ceased to happen. By the time school started the danger was past.

Jack grew into a dog that could have been beautiful, only to me. He was roughly beagle-sized and beagle-shaped, but with no houndlike suppleness. He was rock-hard to the touch, with the musculature of a bull terrier. His toughness was belied, however, by the comic aspect of his ears. One stood upright, German-shepherd fashion, while the other drooped. When people laughed at him, I was torn between welcoming their laughter as a sign of affection toward my dog, and resenting it as ridicule.

In those days the small town where we lived had not yet been engulfed by the nearby city and transformed into a suburb. It was still surrounded by open fields and woods within easy reach of a girl on a bicycle, and a sturdy little brindled mutt. The following summer Jack and I spent every possible moment away by ourselves.

For the first time I knew the heart-filling luxury of having a dependably loving companion. In Jack's company I was free to say foolish things, to act silly, to lie on the grass and roll down a long hill with my dog barking and nipping at my heels all the way down.

In our exploring, we found a seedy old riding stable about three miles from town. We began going there as often as we could, and if I was lucky, I was allowed to lead a few horses to the water trough or perhaps comb a few manes and tails. Jack was indifferent to the horses, but he loved the trips, trotting along the graveled roads beside the bicycle and making side excursions after birds and rabbits.

During cold weather we had to stay close to home, but fortunately the house was large enough to provide getting-away places where baby sisters couldn't follow. It had originally been a funeral home, and in the basement fruit cellar were jars of old embalming fluid. Part of the three-car garage was still used to house the hearse. With Jack beside me for moral support, I got an eerie kind of enjoyment out of playing in the fruit cellar or in the garage with the ominous bulk of the hearse. The garage also served as the stable for my bicycle and the now-outgrown horses built of orange crates and bits of scrap lumber. Even in winter Jack and I could play there for fairly long stretches of time before the cold permeated my cowboy boots and forced us indoors.

But the best place was my room, because no one could come in without my permission, ever. There, with Jack curled hard against my legs, I could lie across the bed and lose myself for hours in my dog and horse books.

The bed served another purpose, too. Whenever special solemnity was called for, usually for taking vows or swearing to secrecy, I stood at the foot of the bed, folded my hands over one high carved bedpost, and rested my forehead on my knuckles. I had stood like this, eyes squeezed shut, when I vowed to break the habit of stealing my church envelope money. I'd find another way to get the pony, I swore, a way less likely to turn me into a criminal.

Jack and I were in the side yard one evening during the summer when Jack was two. I had been throwing sticks for him to chase, pretending not to watch Jan and the older boys shooting baskets on the driveway. Mother and Lois were weeding the small garden under the dining room windows, and my father was attacking dandelions on the front parkway.

A car full of Jan's friends drove by slowly, with much honking and shouting. Jack, sensing a game, ran after it. When the boys saw him, they shouted louder and augmented their calls by pounding on the sides of the car with their palms. To Jack's delight, the noisy thing ran away from him and disappeared around the corner. He came bounding back to me, lopsided ears flapping, tail lashing.

"That's right—you chase them away from here," I said, catching him in mid-leap and hugging him. "Stupid boys, we don't want them around here, do we, old Jack-in-the-Pulpit?"

I threw his stick again, but this time instead of bringing it back, he picked it up, saw another car coming, and cantered to meet it, the stick still in his mouth. For a moment I was terrified that he would be hit, but he stopped short of the street and merely ran along the parkway, keeping abreast of the car and barking a stick-muffled challenge.

I gave little thought to the incident, but when Jack chased each of the next several cars, my father stopped digging and shouted testily, "Lynn, for heaven's sake, make that dog shut up. He'll be bothering the neighbors."

It seemed unlikely to me that anyone could object to so pleasant a sound as my dog's happy bark, particularly since our house was on a corner, and the only neighbors were a grocery store, a gas station, and the Dandee Diaper Service, and it was only eight o'clock in the evening. Nevertheless, the next time a car went by I shouted, "Jackie, no, NO."

He ignored me.

At the approach of the next car I tried to catch his

collar, to hold him until temptation was past, but he sensed a new aspect of the sport and dodged out of reach.

Father muttered, "Darned noisy nuisance."

I had heard those words, that tone, before. Usually they forecasted the end of a pet. The goldfish had been proclaimed nuisances, and the chameleon from the State Fair, and the albino parakeet.

Calling Jack, I went into the house and up to my room to make a vow on the bedpost. "They're not ever going to take you away from me."

All the next day I worked at making Jack understand that he was not to chase cars. He worked at evading me and chasing cars. He was a bright little dog and surely knew he was disobeying, but at the sight of a moving car he seemed to become possessed of a chasing devil, and no matter how hard he was scolded and spanked when I caught him, he did it again and again.

Clenching myself against the look in his eyes, I tied a clothesline to his collar, and when he started after a car, I jerked him off his feet. Eyes dark with hurt, tail tip quivering between his hocks, he came back to me. In every way he could, he apologized. Then another car came and he was off again.

After a morning of rope-jerking he quit trying to chase cars. Elated, I untied the rope. While I was congratulating myself on my ability as a dog trainer, Jack darted up the street to a point where he could run without the rope to hamper him.

For several days the battle grew grimmer, and so did my father, to whom the sound of a barking dog had always been an irritant. At the suggestion of the gas station attendant, who was watching the war from across the street, I tied a rolled-up magazine to Jack's collar in such a way that it dangled and struck his legs when he ran. He enjoyed it.

Someone in Mother's church circle suggested a water pistol, so I tried that. Father ran a fuel oil truck service and had recently bought a Jeep to use around the bulk plant. All one afternoon Mother drove the Jeep back and forth in front of the house while I crouched in the back with a water pistol loaded with vinegar and water, guaranteed to sting Jack's eyes and discourage him from chasing.

But there were problems. Jack, being a town dog and well aware of the danger of running in the street, always stayed on the grassy parkway and so seldom came within shooting range. When he did, my aim was so shaky that only once or twice was he even dampened. The vinegar never got near his eyes. To complicate things further, he soon learned to follow until the Jeep had to slow down for the corner; then he jumped into the back with me. He loved the game.

One afternoon while I was drying the lunch dishes, Jack pushed open the screen door and went outside. I heard a crash, then a scream that became a child's wail of pain and fright.

I flung my towel and ran outside. It was a neighbor

girl, Becky Odland, who was younger than me and very timid. She was sitting in the street under a tangle of bicycle wheels and handlebars. Jack stood near her, cocking his lop-eared head and wagging his tail uncertainly.

"Get him away from me," Becky screeched when she saw me. By this time Jan, Lois, Becky's mother, and, worse yet, my father were converging.

Frantically I tried to pull Becky up from the tangle, but in my haste, I only made things worse.

"He wouldn't hurt you. He's friendly, see?" I pleaded with the little girl to acknowledge that it had not been Jack's fault, and Becky might have admitted it had her mother not swooped down upon her. With this fresh fount of sympathy Becky was off again, sobbing and hiccuping that Jack had chased her and made her fall.

The truth of the matter, as nearly as I could figure it, was that Jack had run alongside the bike, barking, and had startled Becky into swerving and falling. It seemed obvious that the fault was entirely Becky's. But Father's face was ominously dark. By the time he had apologized to Becky's mother, I felt a burning weight of fear in my intestines.

I ate little supper and went to bed early, my arms clamped tight around Jack. His head, which shared my pillow, was damp before we slept.

The next morning Mother suggested that she and I go into town to shop for school clothes. It was late

August, and there had been talk for the past week
about new shoes and blouses. So rarely did mother and
I go anywhere without my two sisters that I was
warmed by the prospect. School clothes meant nothing
to me. They heralded the dreaded confinement of
another school year. But it felt good to be singled out
for the trip.

We caught the ten o'clock bus and were downtown a
half hour later. When the necessary clothes had been
bought, we had lunch in the department store's tea
room, by far the fanciest place I had ever eaten. Then
Mother suggested an early movie. I was surprised.
Ordinarily Mother would be irritable by now with the
pressures of shopping, and anxious to catch the home-
bound bus.

It was after three when we emerged from the theater
and nearly four when we walked the two blocks from
the bus stop to home.

"Jackie, here I am," I called as I barrelled into the
house.

Only silence answered.

So gently that my heart froze, Mother said, "Honey,
Jack is gone."

Explanations ricocheted through my skull. "Your
daddy and I thought Jack would be happier out in the
country....One of Daddy's oil customers on a farm was
wanting a dog....*good* home for him, honey....a
nuisance to the whole neighborhood here..."

I ran up to the bathroom and lost the tea room lunch.

Then I stalked into my room, deliberately letting the
door slam on all of them.

My grief went deeper than the loss of Jack, although
this was pain enough. They had taken not only my dog
but my dignity. I raged, Why didn't they *ask* me? They
had no right.

And below these levels lay another. The act left no
doubt in my logical twelve-year-old mind that my very
real needs meant less to my parents than their fear of
annoying the neighbors.

Days later, when I was able to mention Jack to
Father, I asked him who had my dog.

"A farmer out by Clive, one of my oil customers. You
wouldn't know him."

"I want to go out and see Jack. Tell me the way and
I'll ride my bike. You don't have to take me."

"I don't want you out there bothering them," Father
said. "Just get your mind off that damn dog."

I was astounded. Never before had either of my
parents used even a mild profanity in front of their
daughters. Damn dog, damn dog. The words pierced
my soul and echoed there. He hated my dog this much,
then.

Perhaps some of my emotions showed on my face
because the following Sunday afternoon he relented
and we started out, the whole family, to see Jack. It
was an obvious move to make me feel better, to assure
me that Jack was well and happy. It may have been

some kind of apology. I didn't care what their motives were.

In the back of my mind was a growing possibility. Maybe the farmer's family didn't like Jack after all, and when my folks saw how happy Jack and I were to be back together, they'd change their minds and let me bring him home. I bounced on the car seat so annoyingly that Jan landed a sneak slap on my thigh. I had not even the venom to tattle.

Past the riding stable we went, then down an unfamiliar side road for another four miles. I kept track of the way, planning to ride my bike out to visit Jack as often as possible in case it didn't work out that I could have him back.

As we pulled into the farmyard, I scanned the area for the first sight of a brindled body and lopsided ears. Jack was nowhere in sight. Before the car was fully stopped, I was out, looking in every direction through the welter of sheds and barns and machinery.

A man came out of the house and, ignoring me, shook hands with Father, who was just bending up out of the car.

"This is my daughter Lynn. We were just out for a ride, and she was wanting to stop for a minute to see the dog. I hope it isn't an inconvenient time."

"No, not at all. Glad to have you. Ain't got the little dog anymore, though. That first night after you brought him out, he ran away. Found him clear over by that riding stable, dead in the ditch. Hit by a car, looked like. I figured he must of been trying to find his way home." He paused, then added, "I was awful sorry. He was a nice little dog."

That night Jan made one of her rare visits to the sanctum of my room. She sat on the corner of the bed and said awkwardly. "Listen, Peewee, just remember you're not going to be a kid forever. Someday, before you know it, you'll be old enough to be out on your own. Then you can have all the dogs you want and nobody can ever take them away from you."

After she was gone, I stood at the bedpost in my vow-taking stance.

"That's right," I said. "And I swear someday..."

Goat Lady's Lochinvar

It was nine o'clock on a Friday night in May, a mild night, rich with possibilities.

Spring evening restlessness had pulled me outdoors as soon as the supper dishes were done. I watched from behind the trumpet-vine trellis while my older sister left the house with her date. Then, moodily, I ducked behind the garage and started up the alley toward the elementary school playground two blocks away.

There were friends I could have gone to see, but tonight I preferred to be alone, and to enjoy the sorrow of being alone.

27

The playground was an empty meadow of moonlit gravel. I braced myself in a sprinter's half-crouch, then pelted across the open space at top speed, which was quite fast for a small thirteen-year-old. Arms and legs pumped; chest ached. I slowed but had to catch myself on a rung of the monkey bars in order to stop.

Breathless but tingling, I moved on to the swings, sat on one and twisted around, around, around, around until the chains were wound like a mainspring and the seat raised so high that my foot no longer reached the hollowed dirt and gravel beneath me. Then, relinquishing my body to greater powers, I relaxed and let the swing spin me as it unwound.

For a few moments I sat, arms around the swing chains, head dropping low.

I sang softly to myself as the swing twisted from side to side in response to the shoving toe of my cowboy boot. The boots were getting too small. My toes were curled inside them, and I knew that soon I would be unable to get my feet into them at all. It was a poignant thought. I raised one foot and twisted it for a better look at the scuffed boot with its childishly rounded toe and flat heel. I wondered what ever happened to my Tom Mix glow-in-the-dark spurs that tied on with tassled gold cords.

A movement across the alley caught my attention. It was a large long-haired dog exploring the rim of a garbage can with his nose.

"Here, boy. Here, boy."

I left the swings and held out my hand to him. He was a stranger to me, and I thought I knew every dog in town, certainly every dog in the south half of town. I had been without a dog of my own for several months now, since Jackie was killed, and in that time I had done a thorough job of patrolling the streets and alleys of West Des Moines on one of my stable full of bicycles, holding long conversations with any of the dogs whose owners were liberal about visitors. Not all of them were.

The dog came to me at once, wagging. He had the broad head of an old-fashioned collie and ears that folded back against his skull when I stroked him. He was spotted, brown and very dirty white, and huge felted mats of hair stood out around the base of his ears and over his hips, and dangled from his plumed tail. His eyes were round and dark and mild as he leaned into my hands.

While I talked to him, my hands explored. Under the thick coat was a beadlike row of spine and grotesquely sharp hipbones. His neck bore no collar. Good, I thought. His coat was so dirty that my hands came away darkened and strong-smelling, and in the hollows between his shoulder blades and above the root of his tail, his skin was gritty with black flea droppings as close-packed as grains of sand.

These conditions aroused in me both overwhelming

sympathy and optimism. Clean, well-fed dogs usually belonged to somebody. With this one there was a chance.

"Come on, boy. Let's go home and find you something to eat."

He not only followed me willingly as I started down the alley, but he paced himself close beside me so that my hand rode easily on his head. In my imagination he was clean and well-fed and beautifully groomed, a magnificent animal who was my constant devoted companion, who appreciated me when nobody else did, who risked his life to save mine. For the past month or so I had been reading the Albert Payson Terhune books, and my mind was eager to grasp and expand on any similarity between the dog at my side and the collies who had filled my imagination these past weeks.

From one of these book-dogs I took a name and bestowed it on the dog beside me. "Lochinvar. Your name is Lochinvar." I loved the sound of it.

When we got home, I took him into the garage, knowing that it would be better if my parents didn't see him in his present state. The garage had been built to hold three vehicles, two side by side and a third across the end of the building where double doors opened onto the alley. The two side by side spaces held my father's car and a hearse belonging to a nearby funeral home, which had formerly been in our house and now rented the space from us, but the across-the-rear third of the garage was considered mine. From scrap lumber I had built three stalls there for my bicycles.

My everyday bike, a fairly new light blue and cream one with a sheepskin seat cover, was a black Arabian mare. The second bike, with narrow racing tires, had been my first one. It was too old and battered to have had any trade-in value, especially after I'd painted it dark blue one windy day when a neighbor was mowing his yard, and bits of grass had become imbedded in the damp paint, so I had been allowed to keep it when the newer one was bought. This bike was a Thoroughbred stallion, a retired Derby winner. The third bike was an extremely rusty boy's model given to me by one of my older sister's boyfriends. It was a bay Hackney gelding with plenty of life left in him.

I no longer called them by name, Rusty and Gallant and Black Satin, at least not out loud. I understood that at thirteen I was too old for such foolishness, or for bringing home stray dogs for that matter. But in the darkness of the garage I gave each back fender a pat as I went by.

"You stay here a minute," I told Lochinvar. "I'll be right back with some food, if we're lucky."

Between the garage and the house I stopped and scrubbed my hands on the dew-moistened grass.

Luckily Mother was alone in the living room, knitting and listening to the radio. My father was working in his office off the kitchen, with the door closed. He ran a fuel oil truck service and often did his bookkeeping in the evenings.

"Are you back?" Mother asked, obviously trying not to lose count of her knitting stitches.

"Yeh. Listen, Mother, there's this dog outside..."

She listened with a knowing, resigned expression. "You know he undoubtedly belongs to somebody, don't you?"

"I don't think he does," I insisted. "He's so thin and"—I started to say dirty but changed it to—"lonesome-looking. Can't I just feed him a little bit tonight and see what happens tomorrow? It might save his life."

She gave me a rueful smile that said she didn't believe that any more than I did. "Oh, go ahead, I suppose. There's a little beef stew in the icebox. But don't be surprised if he's gone in the morning."

He was, indeed, gone in the morning. That night he had eaten my offering of stew so greedily and thanked me so warmly with tongue and wriggling, pressing body that when I went to bed there was no doubt in my mind that the dog would stay. But when I ran to the garage at daylight, the small side door stood open a few inches, and Lochinvar was gone.

Saturday mornings held certain invariables. My sisters and I each dusted, straightened and dust-mopped our respective bedrooms in the upstairs of the big white-shingled house, leaving our piles of dust in the hall outside our doors for Mother to collect. We changed the sheets on our beds and sent the dirty ones bombing down the laundry chute from the upstairs bathroom to the basement. After that, my contribution to the general housecleaning was to burn the waste-paper in the alley behind the garage.

I got through all of these stupidities in record time and with minimal care, then set out on Black Satin to look for Lochinvar. Lunch interrupted the search but only temporarily. Then I was off again, systematically covering the grid of streets and alleys, south to Rail-road Avenue, north six blocks to Vine, and east and west from First to Tenth Streets. There was no Loch-invar.

I had swayed Black Satin around the church corner and was coasting toward our garage when I saw him. He was across the street in the alley behind Schultz's Grocery Store, and close beside him was the Goat Lady.

At first I gave no thought to the Goat Lady's nearness to my dog, assuming it was merely coincidence that they were both searching the same garbage piles at the same time. Although I no longer believed the Goat Lady was a witch, as did the younger children of the neighborhood, I decided to stay on my side of the street.

"Here, Lochinvar. Here, boy," I called.

He raised his head from the trash pile, looked in my direction, then came to me in a direct wagging gallop.

Dropping to his level, I wrapped my arms around his neck.

"I knew you wouldn't leave me," I crooned, nearly crying with relief at having found him.

But from across the street came a harsh, metallic voice. "Spotty! Git back here."

The dog left my arms and galloped back, tail thrashing with the pleasure of being wanted on both sides of the street.

I stood up, and from the half shelter of the trumpet-vine trellis, I watched them, my dog and the woman who appeared to be his owner. I knew little about the Goat Lady except that she lived somewhere on the other side of Railroad Avenue and the tracks; that she had, from reports I'd heard, hundreds of animals living with her, mostly goats and cats; and that she was so poor that she had to go around to the grocery stores every Saturday afternoon in search of browning lettuce leaves, carrot tops, and semirotting produce with which to feed herself and her menagerie.

She appeared to be incredibly old, but it was hard to judge because so little of her could actually be seen beneath her year-round costume of a man's overcoat and felt hat, a jumble of long drooping black skirt, and, showing occasionally beneath the skirt, men's galoshes. According to rumor, the hat covered a bald head, but I didn't believe that.

There were other rumors, too—that she was really a man, that she was crazy, that she was part human and

part goat, and so on. Long ago I had discarded all but
the possibility of her being crazy, and I found that
entirely possible and rather interesting.

While I watched, she finished filling her gunnysack
with handfuls of browning greens, and set the sack on
the rusted child's wagon that already held two sacks
from other grocery stores. She took up the wagon
handle, nodded to Mr. Schultz, who waved at her from
the store's back door, and started down the sidewalk
toward Railroad Avenue. Lochinvar walked as closely
beside her as he had, last night, beside me.

I had no plan as I wheeled Black Satin around and
started after her, except that I didn't want to let the dog
out of my sight again. A few doors down the street I
caught up with her and slowed my bike to her gait,
which was so slow that I was forced to cease pedaling
and row myself along with one foot on the curbing.

"Is that your dog?" I asked as pleasantly as I could.
Already I hated the thought of Lochinvar belonging to
her. Any owner other than myself was bad enough, but
the Goat Lady was abhorrent. I forced myself to meet
her eyes and smile when she raised her bowed head
and swung it toward me. This was the closest view I
had ever had of her, and I was encouraged to see that
she had regular human features, similar to the other
old women I knew.

"He's mine, so you just stay away from him," she
rasped.

I had to detour around a parked car, and by the time

I rejoined her I was braced for all-out pleasantness toward the selfish witch.

"I wasn't going to hurt him or anything. I love dogs." We moved on in silence past three or four more houses; then I made another try.

"You wouldn't care if I came over to your house and petted him some time, would you? My folks won't let me have a dog." I was not above using what was a very real sadness, if it would help me win an argument.

The Goat Lady muttered something. The words were lost to me, but their inflection wasn't encouraging.

Two blocks from the corner occupied by my house and the grocery store, the street we were following dead-ended at Railroad Avenue. A weeded embankment faced us. Along its crest ran the Rock Island tracks, and beyond the tracks was an area I had never felt inclined to explore. It held a scattering of tall unpainted wooden houses, dirt paths, and weeds.

Once or twice my older sister and her friends had attempted to tell me what it was that went on in those gaunt curtainless houses, but their explanations always dissolved into giggles, red faces, knowing looks exchanged over my head. I suspected that they didn't really know, themselves, but their attitude was enough to instill in me a feeling of awed curiosity, of distinct uneasiness at the prospect of crossing the tracks. The feeling was heightened by the silent guarded looks that had greeted me the few times I'd mounted the embankment and looked down into the foreign town on the other side.

Now, as the Goat Lady and Lochinvar started up the cinder path toward the tracks, I gripped my courage around me, stood down from my bike, and began wheeling it up the steep slope behind the garbage wagon. Lochinvar trotted back, received my hand on his head, then quickly rejoined the Goat Lady.

She reached the summit, banged her wagon over the tracks, and started down again, but stopped at the sound of my bike jangling across the rails. She turned and stared at me with hard eyes.

"Where you going?"

Beyond her I saw what was evidently her house, a tiny tar paper shack with a dozen or more goats staked out in the weeds around it.

"Could I see your goats?" I asked in my friendliest tone. It was easy enough to sound convincing. I would have enjoyed playing with the dainty stripe-faced nannies and kids.

"You git on home. You got no business over here." She turned away from me and pulled the clattering wagon toward the shack. Lochinvar ranged ahead of her, touching noses with a few of the goats as he went. Obviously he was home.

For a moment I watched from the top of the track bed, hoping against hope that the dog would come to me. He did turn and look up at me, wagging, but the overcoated figure grasped him by the ruff of his neck, and he followed her into the house. Sighing under the weight of life's thousand unfairnesses, I wrestled the bike wheels around on the tracks and coasted down the footpath toward home.

By the time I reached home, my battle plans were drawn. It was intolerable that a great, loving dog like Lochinvar should live in filth on the other side of Railroad Avenue and eat grocery-store garbage. I took the fifty cents I'd been saving toward an hour's ride at the riding stable, and, catching Mr. Schultz just before he closed the store, I bought five cans of dog food.

"You got a dog now?" he asked as he took my money.

Grimly I said, "Not yet but I'm going to."

I hid the dog food in my end of the garage and went in to supper.

In at least one way I was lucky to have the family I had. They accepted the fact that I had affairs of my own that demanded my time outside and were no concern of theirs. Because I never got into trouble and was always home at the expected times, I was allowed a good deal of unquestioned freedom, even after dark. Ours was not the kind of town in which mothers needed to worry about girl children being out at night, although I'm sure my parents did not intend for me to cross Railroad Avenue, even in daylight.

As soon as it was fully dark, I rode to the tracks, going first a block in the opposite direction in case I was being watched. Heart pumping with the danger of what I was doing, I laid the bike down against the cinder embankment and braced my nerves for the climb. I wasn't sure what I was going to do, but I imagined myself as the Lone Ranger closing in on the rustlers, and started up the slope.

A figure appeared at the top. I was terrified, then awash with relief. It was Lochinvar. Either he had known I was there and was coming to me, or else I had been lucky enough to intercept him as he started out in search of food. I believed the second but convinced myself of the first.

"Oh, good dog," I breathed. After a quick hard hug around his neck I remounted Black Satin and pedaled toward home, urging the dog to follow me.

Back in the safety of the garage, sweaty with relief, I stabled the bike and opened one of the cans of dog food with a small thumb-type opener snitched from the silverware drawer while I was drying the supper dishes. In three wolflike snatches Lochinvar finished the can of dog food.

"I wish I could give you more, but I can't afford it."

I rumpled his ears, and with closed eyes he leaned into my hands. "But listen, you come back here every night about this time and I'll feed you again, okay? And then somehow or other I'm going to figure out a way so you can really be mine."

He wriggled hard against me, then slowly settled lower and lower until his head lay across my boot. As I talked on, his tail swept the garage floor in slow arcs.

"She doesn't need you. She's got all those goats and cats and who knows what all, and I don't have anybody. Besides, I can take care of you a hundred times better than she can. I'll feed you regular dog food, the kind that says, Meal of Champions, and I'll get those fleas off of you, and cut the mats out of your hair. Then Mom will let you live in the house and you can even sleep on the foot of my bed."

I made no attempt to shut him in the garage when I finally was called into the house, and I was not surprised that he was gone in the morning. That was all right. The campaign had started.

Nor was I surprised when, the next night, Lochinvar came trotting up the street. I had been waiting on the corner in front of our house, trying vainly to shinny up the street sign pole while I watched for him. When he came, we raced across the yard and into the garage where the can of dog food awaited him. Again we talked until I had to go inside.

Every night the following week Lochinvar came. If I wasn't outdoors waiting for him, he went to the garage door and lay down in the shadows until I appeared.

On Saturday I mowed the yard and earned enough to buy a small can of flea spray at the drugstore, plus three more cans of dog food. That night after Lochinvar had eaten I sprayed him thoroughly with the fragrant stuff, and with the brush left over from my previous dog, I brushed and brushed and brushed. By the time my arm gave out, the floor around patient

Lochinvar was covered with flea corpses and their gritty black specks of debris. Under the damp-brushing Lochinvar's coat became noticeably smoother and shinier. Then, with scissors borrowed under cover from Mother's sewing room, I hacked away the pale wads of matted fur around his ears and on his hips and tail. The effect was rewarding, even in the darkness of the garage with only the moon for a lamp. Lochinvar was still a very long way from being a show collie, or even a regular collie in anyone else's eyes, but now he was respectable and, to me, beautiful.

"You'll feel better now, without those darn fleas biting you," I told him. "See now, if *she* really loved you like I do, she wouldn't have let you get all those fleas on you in the first place. She would have taken better care of you. But don't worry. When I get you, you're going to be the happiest dog in town because I really love you and I know how to take care of you. So please don't go back to her, will you?"

It was with increasing pain now that I watched him go back to the Goat Lady each night. I could see him from my bedroom window as he left the backyard and set off past the grocery store toward his other home. It seemed to me that he should want to stay at my house, that he would hate the thought of going back to her. But still he went.

That night I lay in bed searching for ways to bring Lochinvar closer to me. All the love I could pour on him, plus one can of dog food a night, was doing only a partial job. I wanted to make him *want* to stay with me. It seemed inconceivable that he didn't already have this desire, considering what I offered him in comparison with what the Goat Lady gave him. It was only loyalty to his first mistress that drew him back across Railroad Avenue every night, I told myself. Although I supposed I should applaud his loyalty, it would have been much better if that loyalty were directed to me.

Food was still the only bait I knew, so I decided it would have to be something even more enticing than dog food.

The next afternoon I dragged our lawn mower up the block from house to house until I found a neighbor who would hire me to mow his yard. On any other beautiful Sunday afternoon in spring I would have ridden Black Satin out to the riding stable to hang around envying those who could afford the dollar an hour riding rates. But today there was something more important to do.

That night when Lochinvar came in I was waiting in the open garage door. Some of the fragrance of the flea spray was gone from his coat, but he still looked lovely. Just the absence of the mats was a great improvement.

We went through our hugging and licking ritual; then I dug out the can and can opener, hidden behind an inner tube in the shadowy corner of the garage.

"I earned seventy-five cents today," I told him. "And guess what I'm going to get with it after school tomorrow. Liver! How would you like that, Lochy dear? Would liver be your favorite or would you rather have—"

"Git out of there!"

The harsh command sent my heart into my throat and the can opener clattering to the floor. From the shadow of the trumpet-vine trellis another shadow separated itself; it took the form of a man's crumpled hat and overcoat, a woman's long dragging skirt.

Even Lochinvar looked startled. He had begun to eat his food, but now he raised his head uncertainly and looked from the Goat Lady to me.

Again the voice rasped. "Spotty, git over here."

"I was only feeding him," I said in a voice that wouldn't quite hold firm. "I wasn't hurting him any. You should be glad somebody feeds him."

The Goat Lady came a step nearer. "You was the one to put perfume on him, wasn't you? I reckoned it was you. Now you just stay away from my dog. Little brat."

The insult went unnoticed in my fervor to convince her. "Please, wait, just listen. It wasn't perfume; it was flea spray. The fleas were bothering him, and besides dogs can get tapeworms from fleas. I bought it with my own money, and I've been buying him dog food with my own money, just because I love him. Why won't you let me have him? You don't need him. You've got lots of other pets and he's—"

"He's my dog." The passion in her voice cut through what I was trying to say. Lochinvar went to her, and her old hand shoved his shoulder against her skirt. His tail moved happily.

"If you don't keep away from him, I'm going to git the police on you."

With that rock-hard threat the Goat Lady and Lochinvar moved away, around the corner of the grocery store and out of sight.

Now that she was gone I was thoroughly shaken. I sat on the inner tube, hugging my knees and listening to the Goat Lady's voice bouncing inside my skull. Years ago an older boy had threatened me with the police when I climbed a rose trellis in his backyard. At that time the threat terrified me. For nights afterward I had frightening dreams of policemen and jail. Now I was wise enough to know I couldn't be arrested for feeding someone else's dog. It was not her threat of the police that had set me to trembling; it was the passion with which the threat was made.

Until now I had been working on the assumption that the Goat Lady didn't really care about the dog because she had so many animals. Maybe she *doesn't* really care, I still argued. Maybe it's just that she doesn't want me to have him. She's jealous because he likes me, too.

That seemed not only plausible but highly likely. My conscience receded.

The next day after school I went to a grocery store away from my immediate neighborhood, where the grocers knew I had no dog, and bought seventy-five cents' worth of liver. When I mentioned that it was for my dog, the butcher threw in some rib bones, as I'd hoped he would.

Liver and nice meaty bones, I thought exultantly, coasting down Vine Street hill with the packages bouncing in Black Satin's basket. If he knows he's got bones at my house, he'll want to stay to chew them. I'll tell him they're his bones but that he has to leave them there in the garage to chew them.

That night, as I started out of the house for my rendezvous with Lochy, my father looked up from his newspaper and said, "What do you do out there in the garage every night?"

"I'm working on a project," I said simply. He went back to his reading, and I slipped out the kitchen door, blessing my already established reputation as a person who always has some kind of project going on somewhere.

I waited with the butcher's packages beside me. Sitting on the inner tube, with the small side door open, I could see the corner where Lochinvar would appear. Tonight, I decided, I'd watch to see if the Goat Lady was following. If she was, Lochy and I could escape out the alley doors and hide behind the church's snowball bushes while Lochinvar ate his liver.

But the dog didn't come. I sat, watching, while the paper package in my hand became soggy and my fingers grew sticky with the blood from the liver. It was time to go into the house and still Lochinvar hadn't come. Slowly I unwrapped the liver, left it where he could find it if he came later, and went reluctantly into the house. In my room I shut the door, turned off the lights, put on my pajamas, and then climbed out a window onto the small square porch roof, tucked into a jog in the house. From this perch I could see if Lochinvar came.

With my spine wedged into the corner of the house and my bare feet splayed against the roof shingles, I watched. Some time later I woke, damp with night air, and climbed stiffly back through the window into bed. Lochinvar was not coming.

Nor did he come the next night, or the next. The liver began to smell up the garage and had to be dumped into the garbage can.

She's keeping him from coming, I told myself grimly.

I waited until Saturday afternoon, when the Goat Lady customarily made her rounds of the grocery stores; then I wheeled out the battered old boys' bike from the end stall in the garage. I'd decided not to take Black Satin, for reasons of camouflage and disguise. I rode to Railroad Avenue but stayed one block west of the direct route from my house to the cinder path. On the corner, a block away from the path but within sight of it, I stationed myself beside a tree, mostly out of sight, and waited.

Before long the Goat Lady and her wagon came up over the tracks, down the cinder path, and along the street toward the grocery store. Lochinvar was not with her.

As soon as she was out of sight, I pedaled to the cinder path, dropped the bike against the embankment, and climbed the slope. The pounding of my heart made my movements difficult to control. I wished for the cover of darkness and was, at the same time, grateful for the daylight. On the downhill side of the tracks I met and passed two young men or old boys—I wasn't sure which. They were frightening with their closed faces and hostile eyes that followed me, but I chanted to myself, "Just act like you've got a right to be here."

The shack was nearby, just a few hundred feet from the railroad tracks. It squatted in the sun and the weeds, a black lopsided box about half the size of our garage. I was aware of smells—the goats, rotting garbage, bathroom smells. Trying not to take deep breaths or to breathe any oftener than necessary, I moved among the staked goats toward the shack's one window.

At first I could see nothing through it because of the reflected sun and the dirt on the glass, but by cupping my hands around my eyes I finally made out some shapes inside. The room was an incredible clutter. At first all I could identify was the back of a chair, near me, and beyond that what looked like a corner of a cot. Suddenly something moved. Lochinvar. He tried to stand and come toward me but was halted by a rope tied around his neck and, evidently, to a leg of the cot.

My heart broke for him. I looked toward the door of the shack, wondering if I had the nerve to go inside and free him. But before I could decide I heard a voice behind me.

"What y'all doin' there? Git away from there!"

It was one of the men I'd seen on the path. He had turned and was coming toward me. My brain froze, but my legs took over. I sprinted through the weeds, angled around the man toward the embankment, scrambled up it, and slid down the free side to the waiting bike.

All evening I was tormented by the possibility that the man had told the Goat Lady about me, that she was going to do something worse than just tying Lochinvar in the shack to keep him from me. With a crazy person like her, anything was possible. I didn't bother to go to the garage that night, but went up to my room early and sat brooding on the porch roof.

Again I dozed off and again I woke some time later, but this time I was brought sharply awake by the piercing wail of the fire alarm. I sat up, cracking my head against the shingled wall behind me. A block away, the fire truck went flashing and screaming down Sixth Street toward Railroad. I searched the sky and saw the orange glow somewhere near the foot of our street. Near the Goat Lady's shack, where my dog was tied.

In my haste I fell through the window, taking a good bit of skin off my kneecap. Lights were still on downstairs. My parents stood at the living room window watching the gathering flow of foot and car traffic toward the center of the excitement. The clock said a little after ten.

"I think it's the Goat Lady's house," I said, coming

up breathlessly behind them. "I was watching from the porch roof. Come on, Daddy, let's go down there. Get the car."

They turned to look at me, mildly surprised by my outburst.

"No, we don't want to do that," my father said in his careful way. "We'd just be in the way of the firemen. And it isn't nice to go running off to stare at someone else's troubles."

"I know," I pleaded, "but I've got to find out if it's the Goat Lady. She's got this *dog*, and she keeps him *tied* in the *house*. Please! Or let me go by myself."

They looked at each other; then, with an exhalation of pipe smoke, he relented. "All right, we'll go, but just close enough to find out whose house it is."

Mother said, "Run get your housecoat and slippers and see if the other girls want to go."

After countless delays we were on our way, all five of us in the car, parents in front and daughters in back, as we always rode. I hung out my window, straining to see ahead, while Daddy eased the car slowly down the street, which was fast filling with curious neighbors, many in night clothes.

"Where is it?" I shouted over and over, but it was not until we were nearly to Railroad Avenue that I got an answer. As we approached the corner, a policeman came slowly to intercept our car.

"Can't go any closer," he told my father. "We've got to run hoses across here."

"Whose house is it?" Daddy asked.

"That old lady with all the goats. Looked like she must have knocked over a kerosene lamp or some such. She didn't have electricity in that shack."

"Did the dog get out?" I screamed across my intervening sisters and over the noise. He didn't hear me.

"Did the woman get out okay?" my father asked.

"Afraid not. Well, yes, she got out once, but then somebody said she went back in to get her dog, and the roof collapsed before she could get back out again. Place wasn't anything more than plywood and packing crates, you know. All we're trying to do now is keep the fire from spreading to the other houses."

No one noticed until we reached home that I was soundlessly weeping in my corner of the car. As we walked toward the house, Mother pulled me to her briefly and said, "She was a very old lady, honey. She wouldn't have lived much longer, anyway, and I'm sure the dog was unconscious from the smoke so he didn't feel any pain."

I nodded my head blindly, then shook it and pulled away from her solace. My dog was dead, and I was left with the bitter knowledge that I would not have loved him enough to walk into a burning building for him.

But the Goat Lady had.

Best in Show

It was five o'clock on a snowy Saturday evening in March. I steered the van down into the National Guard Armory parking lot and looked around. "There's Sam's outfit," I said, nodding toward a gray-and-white Volkswagen bus, "and Neila Gorsuch's, and Pete's."

My boss lifted his head from the headrest and glanced around at all the familiar station wagons, vans, and pickup campers. "Hail, hail, the gang's all here," he said drily.

Arthur West was a thin, almost cadaverous man with dark hollows around his eyes and a face that he considered ruggedly handsome. I thought he was homely. He affected an English-country-gentleman aura with his jodphurs and white silk stock, but everyone knew he was really a Wisconsin bartender, or had been before he became a professional dog handler.

I was his crate girl. I was nineteen, and had not yet decided on a profession. The idea of handling show dogs appealed to me, and working for Arthur was an excellent way of learning.

My duties included grooming and caring for the seven dogs that presently made up Arthur's show string, loading and unloading seven heavy dog crates, driving the van from show to show, keeping the books, running errands, and seeing that Arthur was spotlessly turned out and free from dandruff when he entered the show ring. In addition, on secret orders from Arthur's wife, I was to keep him sober, at least until he was through showing, see that he took his vitamins and had a little rest before dinner because of his delicate stomach, and make sure he didn't overdo. There was seldom any danger of Arthur's overdoing.

At the end of the armory I saw a brightly lit garage-sized door standing open. I maneuvered the van through the door and drove into the huge main room of the building.

"Where to?" I asked.

Arthur was roused from his nap now, and his face assumed its show-day look of professionalism.

"Over in that corner there's a kind of cloakroom, if I remember right. Let's get in there if we can."

It was an odd feeling, driving the van indoors, but after two months of being a crate girl I was getting used to peculiarities. I pulled up as close to the cloakroom corner as possible and turned off the ignition.

"Go take a look around," Arthur ordered. "See if Sam and Jeanette are set up yet."

I looked inside the cloakroom, which was quite large and mostly empty. No one was there, but stacked against one wall was a battery of blue-and-silver dog crates in a variety of sizes. They resembled a bank of bus depot lockers. In front of them stood two chrome grooming tables and a semicircle of folding chairs. Sam's stuff.

Good, I thought. Plenty of room in here with Sam and Jeanette, and we'll be out of the way of most of the traffic tomorrow.

Sam was also a professional handler and as close a friend of Arthur's as two handlers ever are, which is not really very close. Arthur specialized in sporting breeds and Sam in terriers, so the two of them were seldom in competition. This helped to keep the friendship alive. So did the fact that they saved on expense money by having Jeanette and me share hotel rooms whenever possible. Jeanette was Sam's crate girl.

Unloading the van was an art that Arthur had down to an ant's eyebrow. He even helped me with it when people were watching. First the folding wire panels of the exercise pen came down from the roof of the van. I set them up in the cloakroom, spread newspapers inside the pen, then began releasing the dogs into the pen, two by two, from their crates in the back of the van. While each pair of dogs was getting the kinks out of their legs, I wrestled their crates out of the van and into the cloakroom. Before the job of unloading reached this heavy stage, Arthur wandered off to talk to someone.

When all the dogs were unloaded, exercised, watered, and tucked away in their crates again, I began mixing the seven huge pans of food.

"Hey, you got here." It was Jeanette, with Sam close behind her.

She was a large girl in her late teens, with a broad Scandinavian face and long braids of off-white hair. She looked like a stereotype of sturdy peasant stock. Sam was nearly a head shorter than Jeanette, a bow-legged Irishman of indeterminant age. Sam was a perfectionist with his dogs and a man who never let moral considerations stand in the way of a good time or a win in the show ring. One might dislike Sam in retrospect, but in his presence it was impossible to resist his spirit of fun.

We had all been together just the previous weekend at the Detroit show so there was little news to catch up on, but with Sam there was never a lull in the conversation.

"Who have you got?" he asked, peering into Arthur's seven crates.

"Same string. We're hoping to finish the little Irish setter bitch this time. She only needs two more points. And possibly the springer." I began opening crate doors and sliding pans of food in to my waiting charges.

"How about you?" I asked.

"Same." Jeanette said. "Oh, no. We've got a new little Welsh pup, but he's not in very good coat yet."

I finished the feeding and opened the top end crate on Sam's stack. "Hi, Penny. How's my girl?"

The dog inside leaped out and into my arms. She was a miniature schnauzer, the most beautiful one I had ever seen, with a charcoal coat edged in spun silver. Her name was American and Canadian Champion Shadow Glen Tuppence, and she was Sam's top dog, his one hope for Best in Show. She already had seven Best in Shows to her credit, and I knew Sam would not have bothered to come to a show as small as this one if he weren't reasonably sure of adding another top victory to Penny's record. With Penny, Sam had a chance at the coveted designation of Handler of the Year, and one more Best in Show would just about clinch it.

A dog show is a large-scale process of elimination, beginning with individual classes within each breed, such as Puppy, Open or Bred by Exhibitor, with each of these subdivided by sexes. Winners of each class compete for Winners Dog and Winners Bitch, then go for Best of Winners and Best of Breed. The hundred or so Best of Breed dogs then compete for Best of Group, that is, Hounds, Terriers, Toys, and so forth. Finally the Group winners compete for the supreme victory, Best in Show.

Although individual owners are usually content with winning a class or perhaps Best of Breed, for the professional handlers like Arthur and Sam the fight doesn't really begin until the Best of Group and Best in Show competition. Penny was the first top dog Sam had ever handled, and to a great extent his reputation depended on her continued success.

The little dog wriggled in my arms and thrust her mustachioed muzzle into my ear. I knew that tomorrow no one but Sam and Jeanette would be allowed to touch her coat so she and I did our playing now.

Jeanette said, "Penny's owner is coming down for the show tomorrow. He's from Minneapolis. A Cadillac dealer, I think."

She had hoisted Balthazar onto the grooming stand and was hand-feeding him. Balthazar, the only non-terrier in Sam's string, was a massive red-and-white Basset hound who was perfectly capable of eating by himself. But he had long ago learned that if he refused to eat before a show Jeanette would spend a great deal of time rolling his food into moist egg-sized balls and poking it down his throat, talking to him and petting him as she worked. It was a lot of fun for Zar, a guaranteed attention-getter, and Jeanette, who dared not let him become thin just before a show, went along with the hunger-strike tactics. Zar sat watching me from the corners of his woeful eyes, moving his tail slowly as he relished Jeanette's attention.

Sam handed me a show catalog pilfered from the superintendent. It listed all the competing dogs.

"Okay, Sam," I said, leafing through the catalog. "Who's it going to be for Best in Show tomorrow? No, don't tell me—let me guess." I scanned the four-hundred entries, looking only at the dogs with the prefix of Champion before their names. These would be the serious contenders.

"Hmmm, there's Penny, of course. Neila Gorsuch's Yorkie or—Weatherly's Afghan or—who else?"

"No contest," Sam snapped. "The Afghan's already got it."

It was unlike Sam not to elaborate so I prodded him. "How do you know? He's got a couple Best in Shows, but they were just small ones in the South. Penny's record..."

Sam's face turned hard. He glanced around the room with the stealth of a third-rate spy although we three were alone. Then, looking at Jeanette, he motioned with his head toward the main room. I put Penny back into her crate and followed him, curious. I'd never seen Sam act this way before.

In the huge main room of the armory crews from the Indiana Dog Shows Company were unloading a van full of folding chairs, loudspeaker equipment, ropes and standards with which to mark off the six judging rings, and huge rolls of rubber matting. Several of the workmen were familiar to me by now. I waved and returned their half flirtatious greetings.

Sam led the way to the corner where the ladies of the local kennel club were setting up tables from which to sell food and beverages tomorrow. Although they weren't yet open for business, Sam sweet-talked them out of two paper cups of coffee. We sat on a dog crate that stood alone against the wall. No one was near us for the moment.

"For heaven's sake, what's with the Afghan?" I demanded.

Sam studied me with his pale little eyes. "Can you keep your mouth shut?"

"Well, of course I can."

He took a sip of coffee. "Shaw is judging Best in Show," he said. Doom rang in his tone.

"So?"

"It was supposed to have been Garrity, but at the last minute they switched it to Shaw."

"I don't understand the problem. What's wrong with Mr. Shaw judging Best in Show? Has he got something against Penny?"

Sam gave me a look I had come to know and hate during my brief crate-girl career. The look said, "You're a kid; you haven't been around the shows long enough to know zilch. Only us old-timers who've been in the business for years are entitled to an intelligent opinion."

"What's wrong with Shaw," Sam explained patiently, "is that Weatherly is here with his Afghan."

Again I looked blank.

Sam went on. "Norbert Weatherly and Pierce Shaw are very old and very close friends, from way back when Shaw was a handler and the two of them used to work together. So when Shaw first applied for his judge's license, there was a little trouble—it's too complicated to explain to you—but Weatherly had some influence with the A.K.C. and he managed to pull some strings to get Shaw's license approved. See? So now any time Shaw is judging Best in Show and Weatherly gets a Group win, it's an automatic Best in Show for old Norbert."

I was naively indignant. "But that's not honest, Sam."

He merely shrugged. "Fortunes of war, kid. Fortunes of war. Come on, let's go round up the gang and get some supper. There's a good little steak place just down the highway. I remember it from last year. And listen, don't go spreading this around, remember."

I raised my paper cup in a pledge of secrecy.

When I arrived at the show building at six the next morning, our cloakroom held two more clusters of equipment—the varnished wood crates of Neila Gorsuch, who handled only toy breeds, and the battered, nondescript stack belonging to Johnnie Herbert. Johnnie would not be along until the last possible moment, but his crate girl, Florence, was already hard at work filling water pans from a nearby faucet.

Florence was a short stout woman in her fifties with mannish gray hair and a chin that I'm sure she shaved every morning. She was strident, overbearing, and fond of her role as a character.

We exchanged greetings as I began letting my dogs out, two by two, into their exercise pen. First came Mac, the huge champion Irish setter, then Bridget, a fine-boned young Irish bitch.

"How's Johnnie?" I asked. This was always good for a dialogue of at least ten minutes from Florence.

"Terrible, terrible," she said, predictably. "Crazy fool was out yesterday in all that slush running the dogs. Got his feet just soaked. Anybody that's got size thirty feet like he's got and don't have sense enough to keep 'em dry ought to be shot."

"Catch cold, did he?" I turned away because I couldn't keep the amusement from my face.

"Cold! Worst darn cold the world has ever seen. Crazy fool. But I made him tie a dirty sock around his neck last night before he went to bed. That's the best cold cure there is, did you know that? Dirty sock around the neck."

"No, Florence, I didn't know that."

Jeanette joined us. At the sound of her voice every dog in the blue-and-silver crates set up a cacophony of joy.

"Oh, listen, Jeanette," I said, fishing a bottle of

whiskey from the bottom of Arthur's tack trunk, "would you hide this for me someplace till after the show? I've got strict orders from Arthur's wife."

"Sure." Jeanette nodded toward the large bottom-tier crate that housed Balthazar. "Zar will watch over it. He's a guaranteed teetotaler."

I got down on all fours and crawled into the crate with the delighted Basset. In the far corner, under a pile of shredded newspapers that formed Balthazar's bed, I buried the bottle.

"You guard that with your life," I warned the dog. "If Arthur comes looking for it, you sit on it and growl."

"Who are you betting on for Best in Show?" Florence asked. Her voice was strained with the effort of boosting a Saint Bernard onto her grooming table. She pinned a towel around the dog's neck to keep his chest dry, and set about washing the folds of his face.

"Penny, of course," Jeanette said. "No, seriously, I'd say it'll be between Penny and the Afghan."

I glanced at her, wondering if she knew what I knew.

"Nah," Florence said. "There's a parti cocker here from New York, been piling up Best in Shows like poker chips on the Florida circuit. I say it'll be him. How about you, Lynn?"

"Oh," I said thoughtfully, "that's an awful nice Afghan. I think he'll take it." That was not giving away any secrets, I thought, and it would be nice to be able

to say I told you so after the Afghan won. I'd never yet
guessed right.

It was nine o'clock and time for the judging to begin
before Sam, Arthur, and Johnnie Herbert came strol-
ling into the cloakroom.

Johnnie was, in his own way, even more of a
character than Florence. He worked harder at it. He
was a huge messy man with thinning hair and a glass
eye that he regarded as a valued part of his image. In
addition to the regular glass eye he ordinarily wore, he
carried a spare that was etched with fine red lines. On
the frequent mornings when he was feeling the effects
of the previous night's drinking, he wore the bloodshot
glass eye so that it would match his real eye. One of his
favorite jokes was to drop whichever eye he wasn't
wearing into someone's drink when the victim wasn't
looking.

"How's your cold?" I asked him as I moved over to
make room for Arthur behind the grooming table
where I was working on Mac's paws, trimming around
the pads of his feet with small curved scissors.

"Fine, all gone," Johnnie boomed.

I said to Arthur, "Dirty sock around the neck—that'll
do it every time."

We began in earnest now, all six of us, to groom
whichever of our dogs was scheduled for judging first.
For Arthur and me it was the two Irish setters. Because
Bridget was slightly smaller than she should have
been, it was my job to take her into the ring and show
her, while Arthur stayed out of sight. It was legal for a

crate girl to show a client's dog when the handler was
unable to do so, and although Arthur could have
shown Bridget, he was going on the theory that she
looked larger standing beside short me than she would
have beside him. It seemed to work.

Bridget won her class and Winners Bitch, and Mac
won Best of Breed. Hurriedly now, Arthur and I went
to work on the two Labrador retrievers and the
springer spaniel. The morning passed in a frenzy of
grooming, listening to the loudspeaker calling classes,
trotting from crates to ringside and back to crates. By
lunchtime all of our dogs had had their moment of
glory or defeat, and we were able to relax.

I bought a cup of pop and a partially warmed hot
dog, and ambled slowly around the rings, watching the
judging and listening to bits of conversation.

"...so I said to him, 'Well! You can't be much of a
judge if you can't even recognize a scissor-bite when
you see it, for God's sake...'"

"...paid twelve-hundred dollars for an English import, sight unseen, my dear, and when the dog
arrived..."

"...never going to show under Garrity again. He's so
old he can barely creak across the ring, and the man's
ninety-percent blind, you know. One time he thought
he was judging a class of Irish water spaniels and he'd
disqualified the whole class for being undersized
before he found out the class was *American* water
spaniels."

"...are saying Best in Show is in the bag for the

Afghan of Weatherly's. I've heard it from several
people, so it must be true. Something about the judge
owing a favor to the handler. I don't know what these
dog shows are coming to. Back in my day..."

I stopped in mid-bite, then walked away with the
same unreasonable guilt with which drivers glance at
their speedometers when a police car comes into view.
I knew, when I stopped to think, that I had not let the
secret out. Sam must have confided in someone else, or
possibly the situation was known to someone besides
Sam. At any rate the word was obviously out now. I
went back to the cloakroom.

Sam was just returning Penny to her crate and
tucking the Best of Breed trophy into the bottom of his
tack trunk. Arthur was there too, looking around with a
puzzled expression and stroking his white silk stock.

"I can't figure out where it went to," he said plain-
tively. "Lynn, have you seen my bottle of Scotch? I
was sure I packed it."

"Someone probably swiped it," I said.

Sam put his arms around Jeanette and me, and
steered us toward the cloakroom door. "Why don't you
girls go walk around a little. Find out what the
competition is going to be for the Terrier Group. I've
been too busy to mark my catalog."

We went, moving with seemingly aimless leisure
around the main room, which was now packed with
dogs, crates, and slowly moving clots of people. After a
full tour we decided the only threat to Penny for the

Group was the West Highland White terrier. We sought out the dog and found him standing on his handler's grooming table while the handler lounged beside him, talking to someone.

I stared at the Westie, pretending to evaluate him but actually knowing very little about the breed. Jeanette took a more direct approach. While the handler was looking the other way, she reached out and brushed her fingertips over the dog's rear. The Westie jumped and spun toward her.

His handler turned and gave Jeanette a dirty look.

"Sorry," she said. "He sure is a dandy."

We moved on. All the way back to our own territory I wondered whether craftiness was contagious. Jeanette had always seemed such an honest, forthright girl before she began working for Sam.

We reported back to headquarters, and Jeanette read off the list of Best of Breed terriers. "The Westie is the only one you have to worry about," she said, "and he's touchy in the rear."

Supper was barbequed ribs and baked beans, sold by the kennel club ladies. The six of us, including Johnnie and Florence, pushed our grooming tables together, covered them with newspapers, and picnicked.

"I sure wish I could figure out what happened to that bottle of Scotch," Arthur moaned. "This coffee tastes like bath water."

In his crate Balthazar stirred up his nest of shredded newspapers and resettled himself.

After supper we went out to watch the Group judging, except for Sam, who was putting superfluous finishing touches on the patient Penny, and Arthur, who was waiting with Mac for the announcer to call the first group, Sporting Dogs.

The crowd had thinned considerably by now, and the six small rings had been consolidated into one large one. Down the center was a row of placards naming each of the sporting breeds. The class was called, and the room became still.

Into the ring swept Arthur and Mac, followed by the others setters, pointers, retrievers, and finally the smaller spaniels. It was a good class and a large one, and it seemed to take an endless time for the judge, Mr. Shaw, to select the parti-colored cocker for first place. Mac was fourth, which was more than Arthur had hoped for.

When the Terrier Group was called, Sam and Penny jockeyed into position just behind the West Highland White. As the dogs began to circle the ring, I suddenly understood what Sam was doing. He gradually increased his speed until Penny was at her best gait. But the short-legged Westie could go no faster without breaking into a run, which would make him look bad. Sam refused to go out around the Westie, as he ordinarily would have done, and every time the Westie felt Penny crowding him from behind he spun around and snapped at her.

I felt slightly sick.

First place went to American and Canadian Champion Shadow Glen Tuppence, miniature schnauzer. Second place went to the West Highland White, an equally good dog but obviously lacking in ring manners.

The rest of the Group judging dragged on until at length the six winners were declared: the parti cocker, Penny, Weatherly's regal black Afghan, a Shetland sheepdog, Neila Gorsuch's Yorkie, and a black standard poodle.

Into the ring they came, and once again the room was still. The climax was now at hand.

With only six dogs to choose among, the elimination went fairly rapidly. First the Shelty and the poodle were motioned to one side, and then the Yorkie and the cocker. Only the Afghan and Penny were left standing like carvings in the center of the ring. The little charcoal schnauzer had never looked more beautiful or moved with more dash and precision. My heart broke for her; I knew that she understood the difference between victory and defeat, that she was striving for the loving fuss that came with winning, and that she had no chance.

Suddenly Mr. Shaw took from his table the huge silver loving cup and handed it to Sam. I stared.

Jeanette was shouting and pounding my back, but in
spite of the excitement of the moment I was caught by
the expression on the judge's face. From where I stood
he seemed to be controlling a furious anger. His face
was tight and flushed.

While Sam was detained in the ring for photographs
and congratulations, I went back to my dogs and
began getting things squared away for the night. We
wouldn't start the long drive home until morning.

Arthur wandered in. "Sure wish I had a drink. I'm
worn to a frazzle."

I got down on my hands and knees and crawled into
Balthazar's crate. "Oh. Guess what I found," I said,
emerging with the bottle. Balthazar had chewed off the
label, but Arthur didn't notice. He merely gave me a
dirty look and went to work on the cork.

An hour later twelve of us were seated at a table in
the town's finest restaurant. Although most of us had
already eaten one dinner, tradition demanded that the
Best in Show winner treat his friends after the show,
and Sam was a magnanimous victor. He sat on one side
of me, and on the other side, on the chair between
Jeanette and me, sat Penny. She was a celebrity tonight, and the management's objections were swept
away by the exuberance and heavy tipping of Penny's
owner.

All of us, including Penny, were eating our way
through thick mushroom-smothered steaks. In the cen-

ter of the table sat the silver loving cup filled with cracked ice from the restaurant's kitchen and bristling with gleaming bottles of pink champagne.

To the delight of the entire room full of people Jeanette poured a glass of champagne and held it down while Penny lapped, paused, licked her whiskers, and then licked the glass dry.

In the lull I leaned close to Sam's ear and whispered, "See? The dog game isn't as crooked as you thought. The Afghan didn't get it after all."

Sam laughed, louder and longer than I thought necessary. "You got a lot to learn, kid," he said finally.

Immediately I was on the defensive. "What do you mean by that?"

From the corner of his mouth Sam murmured, "Where do you think that story got started anyway, about Weatherly and Shaw?"

I raised my eyebrows and he nodded.

"But why?" I was thoroughly confused.

"Use your head, girl." He gestured with a forkload of steak and dropped a mushroom onto the tablecloth. "I whisper a few well-chosen words to three or four gossipy broads, tell them to keep it a secret, and an hour later it's all over the show building. First thing you know it gets back to the judge, and what's he going to do? He goes into that ring knowing everyone watching him has heard that he's going to put up the Afghan for personal reasons. The man's on the spot, see? No way he can prove it isn't true, and if he gives it to the Afghan, everybody assumes it *is* true. And there goes his reputation as an honest judge. So he plays it safe and gives it to somebody else. Smart, huh?"

I put down my fork. The steak suddenly wasn't very good. I thought about Penny doing her honest best in the show ring week after week; I thought about the magnificent black Afghan, who had tried equally hard and equally blindly to win the attention and praise that came with victory.

"Yes. Very smart, Sam."

I turned away from him and from all the other loud-voiced celebrants, and drew Penny up close to me. She licked my wrist.

Cowardly Kate

Some dogs live out their lives without ever seeing their owners. They are born, raised, exhibited, bred, retired, and buried at the kennel of a professional handler or trainer. Often the owners are wealthy people whose life-styles are incompatible with dog ownership but who have a genuine love for either fine dogs or perhaps well-filled trophy cases.

Klondike Kate was one such dog. Her legal owner was a Philadelphia industrialist, but she had no knowledge of his existence. Her entire three years had been spent in the fourth run on the right, in the kennel of Arthur West, professional handler of show dogs, sporting breeds a specialty.

For a golden retriever Kate was small—at least she gave the appearance of being small, partly because she spent every waking moment in a frightened crouch. When the door from her pen to her run was opened, she bolted in or out, in terror of being touched. If a person stood above her and looked directly down into her eyes, the tension was enough to send her spinning in a frenzy at our feet.

To my almost certain knowledge, Kate had never in her life been mistreated or spoken to in a harsh tone. The only humans she had any contact with at all were Mr. or Mrs. West or myself, and all three of us were dog lovers of the highest order. Kate's was a classic case of kennel shyness. It happens sometimes to a dog who has inherited a tendency toward excessive shyness and who, in those crucial first weeks of life, does not receive a great deal of human socializing.

I was working that spring for Arthur West, helping with the kennel work and, on weekends, assisting him on the dog-show circuits, so for those months most of Kate's care fell to me. With twenty setters, pointers, and retrievers to take care of, I had little time to spend with the hopelessly neurotic Kate, but because I was too young to have learned my limitations, and because I had romantic notions of the power of love, I did try to break down Kate's fear.

After the other dogs were fed, brushed, and turned out by pairs into the orchard for their exercise, and

after all the runs had been cleaned, hosed, and disinfected, and after Arthur had given me my daily
lesson in such arts as how to pose a thin-fronted dog to
hide the fault or to razor-trim an Irish setter's throat so
that it didn't looked trimmed, I worked with Kate.

I crawled into her pen and sat on the wooden
bed-platform while she cowered in the far corner. I
sang "K-K-K-Katy" in what I hoped was a low, reassur-
ing voice, and let my hand touch her paw or her tail
tip. No response. I tried staying in her pen when I
brought her pan of food, but she refused to eat in my
terrifying presence.

When my period of employment was over and it was
time to leave, Kate and I were not one fraction closer
than we had been on the day I arrived.

On a golden morning in early June I began packing
my old Chevrolet for the trip toward a destination as
yet undecided. I hoped to find another job with a
professional handler because I wanted to learn the
business, but as yet I had had no firm job offers.

From house to car I went, back and forth, jamming
the trunk with boxes and bags of personal belongings.
I was in a low mood. This had been a pleasant job,
often grindingly hard but filled with dogs, dog lore,
and learning. I'd have been sorry to leave even if I had
known where I was going.

Just as I finished stuffing the car trunk, Arthur came
up the drive from the mailbox. He was walking slowly,
reading a letter as he came.

On the third attempt I was able to slam the trunk lid

hard enough for the latch to catch and hold. I turned
and waited for Arthur to come and tell me good bye,
wish me luck, say I'd done a good job, something.

What he said was, "Got a letter from Kate's owner."
He waved the sheet thoughtfully. "He says I should go
ahead and have her put to sleep. Kind of hate to..."

"Why does he want to do that?" I demanded, knowing the answer.

"Why, hell, she's not ever going to be any good for
showing, as shy as she is, and I'd sure never use her for
breeding. I can see his point. He's put out a lot of
money for her board all these years. Listen, Lynn, why
don't you take her? See if you can do anything with
her. Sometimes dogs like that will come out of it if you
make house pets out of them."

I hesitated. I had very little money, no job in the
offing, and if I was lucky enough to find work in
another kennel there would almost certainly be a ban
against my keeping a dog of my own. As far as I could
see, Kate was hopeless anyhow. I couldn't imagine any
amount of socializing curing her at this advanced stage
of her neurotic development.

But on the other hand if it meant saving her life...
Besides, it would be nice to have a companion as I set
out to seek my fortune, even a companion like Kate.

"Sure, I'd be glad to take her."

Ten minutes later we were on our way, Kate and I.
Arthur had given me Kate's pedigree, which was
almost solid bench and field champions, and had even

donated an old nylon show lead and a paper sack of
dog meal.

Kate was not much company. All morning she remained pressed against the back floor between my
typewriter and a carton of old dog magazines Arthur
had discarded. We were traveling south through Wisconsin on little-traveled blacktop highways that wandered among deep-green pine and birch forests.

The destination for tonight was a town in northern
Illinois where tomorrow there was to be a sanctioned
match, an informal dog show primarily for the benefit
of pups and inexperienced exhibitors, a sort of dry run
for regular dog show competition. I had promised to
come to the match to help a friend who had five corgis
to show and too few relatives to handle all of them.

Kate and I stopped for lunch at a drive-in root-beer
stand so that I wouldn't have to leave her alone in the
car. After much coaxing I was able to get her out and
lead her to a grassy area, but she was too frightened to
take advantage of the opportunity to relieve herself.

By midafternoon the car was uncomfortably warm. I
opened the windows on the far side a couple of inches
and rolled mine all the way down. I was stiff from
sitting, and it felt good to be able to rest my arm on the
opened window and shift my weight a little.

Suddenly something struck the back of my head,
knocking it against the steering wheel. The car was
going at highway speed and very nearly careened into
the ditch before I was able to get hold of it again. I

pulled off the road and turned around just in time to
see Kate streaking across an open field, her lead
lashing the air behind her.

"Oh, bad word, bad word," I fumed. "If that's the
way you want it, you just go ahead and run away. Who
wanted you in the first place, you neurotic spook? I've
got to get to Rockford by tonight. I can't spend all
afternoon chasing you."

I locked the car and, of course, spent all afternoon
chasing her.

She was out of sight by the time I had wriggled
through the barbed-wire fence. It was a pasture, a very
large pasture from the looks of it, and even a city girl
like me could tell there were cows in residence. I
plodded straight ahead through the hummocks of long
grass, keeping one eye out for a flash of gold, another
for the cattle and the nearest fence. Cattle per se didn't
frighten me, but one could never tell about bulls or
about calves' mothers.

About the time I was seriously considering leaving
the darned dog to her chosen destiny, I came to the
bank of a stream. There, about five feet out and belly
deep in muddy water, stood Kate. Her expression was
foolish, pitiful, and thoroughly hangdog.

"Okay, girl, come on out," I coaxed. Her head
drooped lower.

"Oh, honestly." I kicked off my tennis shoes, rolled
up my pant legs as far as they would go, which wasn't
very far, and waded in. As my feet sank into the muddy

bank, I thought about water snakes, crawdads, all the stinging, biting, and pinching things that might be living in the ooze. I expected Kate to retreat from my grasp, but when I caught the trailing lead and said, gently but firmly I hoped, "All right, come on out now," she came.

She stood patiently and without spinning while I tried to wipe the worst of the mud from both of us with a handful of grass, and she followed meekly all the way back to the car.

It was a turning point, of sorts, in our relationship. We were not yet friends, but it seemed that she had concluded that I was perhaps the lesser of the evils that surrounded her.

At the sanctioned match the next day Kate stayed in the car, occasionally daring to raise her head high enough to peer out the windows. The match was held in a well-shaded park and there was not much of a crowd, so I didn't worry about leaving her in the car.

When the corgis had been shown, I told my friend about Kate. "Why don't you show her just for the heck of it, as long as she's here?" the woman said. "They're doing sporting breeds in about an hour. We'd have time to get her brushed up."

At first I declined, thinking of Kate's delicate psyche, but finally curiosity overcame caution and I went to the card table where entries were being taken. I had Kate's pedigree with me, and sanctioned matches are relatively informal affairs, so there was no problem about getting her entered.

We took Kate from the car and set her up on my friend's grooming stand. Kate was somewhat accustomed to this from the routine at Arthur's kennel, and she seemed less frightened by the surroundings than I had anticipated.

Most of yesterday's mud had dried and fallen off by now, but we brushed out the rest of it. Then I went to work, cautiously, trimming around the pads of her feet and rounding off her tail tip. Bushy hunks of pale yellow fur stood up in front of her ears, making the ears look unattractively high, but when I tried to trim them she began cringing and shaking, so I decided not to press my luck.

"Who's judging retrievers?" I asked as I brushed.

"Glen Aberfeldy."

"Oh."

The judges at sanctioned matches are not regulation dog show judges but are usually local professional handlers such as Arthur West. I didn't know anything about Glen Aberfeldy.

"He should be good," said my friend from the other side of Kate. "He's applied for a license to judge sporting breeds. Going to give up handling and become a full-time judge just as soon as his license is approved."

Bully for him, I thought. I was beginning to dread going into the ring with Kate. She'd be too frightened to gait properly if I could get her around the ring at all, and she almost certainly wouldn't stand calmly for the judge's close examination.

I was right. She balked all the way around the ring, pressing herself against my legs in a pitiful attempt to disappear. Mr. Aberfeldy took one look at her and said, loudly, "That dog has no business in a show ring." He gave the first and second-place ribbons to the only other dogs in the ring but declined to award Kate third place in a class of three. This was the ultimate insult a judge could give.

Kate and I left the ring and the match and the town, united suddenly in an us-against-them fury. At least that was my mood. Although I had been more than half convinced, myself, of Kate's worthlessness before the match, I certainly wasn't going to let any stupid non-judge insult us that way. After all, Kate wasn't that bad.

The money ran out, jobs eluded me, and eventually Kate and I went to my parents' home in Iowa. I took a job writing radio commercials for a small local station, and in my spare time I continued to work with Kate.

By now she accepted me but was still terrified of other people, loud noises, strange places, sudden movements. Her affection for me had the same desperate quality as that of a dying man's for proof of a hereafter.

I wrote to Kate's legal owner and explained the

situation to him. His answer was to send me Kate's registration, signed over to me, and to say that he was delighted that she had a good home.

Gradually the weeks passed and Kate relaxed just the slightest bit. She was able to eat without bolting her food and vomiting it later, so she gained weight. With daily brushing and treats of bacon fat, her golden coat began to gleam. I was allowed certain liberties now, so the ear tufts were removed and her toenails were trimmed. She seemed to grow taller, too, because she no longer crouched.

Part of the rehabilitation program was to take her, each evening after work, to the town square and make her sit quietly beside me while traffic swished by and strangers passed. At first she spent the entire time cringing against my knees, but after several weeks she began to relax. She still hated it, but not quite so much.

In August Doc Petry called from his home near Chicago. Doc was not a doctor at all: he was a dog handler I had gotten to know while traveling the circuits with Arthur West. He was planning to make the Kentucky circuit, he said, and his crate girl had just quit, leaving him without help. Would I be interested in working those shows for him? Regulation pay and room for one more dog on the load, if I had one I wanted to bring.

"I sure would be interested, and yes I do have a dog I'd like to show, a golden retriever."

We agreed on the details, and I hung up, elated at the

chance to get back into the fray and to see what Kate would do now.

"Are you ready to give it another try?" I asked her as I made out her entry blank. She thumped the floor with her tail and pressed close to my legs.

"Well," I said with a sigh, "I guess you're as ready as you'll ever be."

It was a three-show circuit over the Labor Day weekend, beginning at Lexington, Kentucky, and ending at Louisville. The Lexington show was held on the grounds of the beautiful Keenland Racetrack.

Like most of the other exhibitors, Doc and I set up shop in the broad alleyway of the most storybooklike stable I'd ever seen. It was built of dark weathered brick and oak beams, and it smelled of clean straw and neat's foot oil. There were no horses in residence that day, to my disappointment.

Most of Doc's dogs were shown in the morning, so I had the afternoon free to put finishing touches on Kate. She was taking the whole thing with relative aplomb, only trembling and salivating a little inside the dark and roomy crate Doc had provided for her.

An hour before her class was called I realized that I hadn't even checked to see who was judging goldens. Some professional I was. After all, knowing the preferences of the various judges was one of the most important tools in a professional handler's bag of tricks. If a certain judge was a stickler for proper tail carriage, you didn't show your gay-tailed collie under him. And so forth. I didn't yet know much about any of the judges, but I went through the motions anyway and looked up the golden retriever judge in my show catalog.

Golden retrievers, four o'clock, ring one, Glen Aberfeldy, judge, I read.

"Oh, my Lord."

"What's the matter?" Doc said as he approached with two paper cups of Seven Up.

"Thanks. I need that." I took one cup and drank. "I just found out the judge who's doing goldens is the same guy who, just last June, told me Kate had no business in a show ring. She was third in a class of three at a cussed *sanctioned* match, and he withheld the ribbon."

Doc was thoughtful for a moment. "Does he know you?" he asked finally.

"No. Saw him just that one time, and I don't think he paid much attention to me. Why?"

Doc was looking at my shoulder-length hair. "How would you like a haircut?"

For an instant I was confused, but then I understood what he was thinking. If Mr. Aberfeldy recognized me, he was bound to remember Kate, and his first impression of her. She wouldn't have a chance at an impartial opinion today.

In a few minutes, I was perched on Doc's grooming crate, with a dog towel around my shoulders, while he

went at my hair with his dog shears. He did a surprisingly good job, probably from all his practice with
poodles. Twenty minutes later my hair was reduced to
a length of about two inches all over. Doc even wet the
comb in a drinking fountain and shaped my hair into a
more or less fashionable gamin style. The change in
my appearance was rather exciting, and was surely
enough to fog any memory Mr. Aberfeldy might have
had of a long-haired girl and a cringing retriever seen
briefly three months ago.

When our class was called, Kate followed me to
ringside with only a suggestion of hesitancy in her
gait. I dared to hope.

It was a large class of golden retriever bitches, at
least for this part of the country—five besides Kate. I
glanced at the others briefly. A strong class. A couple
of nothings, but the others would be competition.

Kate and I led into the ring on the moot theory that
the first dog in might have a very slight psychological
advantage. Kate gaited well, and when the time came
to line up for examination, she held her pose like a
statue. But I could feel, through the lead, that she was
trembling.

Mr. Aberfeldy began his examination at the far end
of the line. Contrary son of a gun, I muttered to myself.
Kate's trembling grew more and more pronounced as
the seconds passed. I kept up a steady murmur of
encouragement. She watched me from the corner of
her eye. The terror was growing. When neither Kate

nor I could have borne the tension another moment,
Mr. Aberfeldy came to stand before Kate's head. She
was about to start spinning. I could feel it.

He reached slowly for her head. Every muscle in
Kate's body turned to iron. Her heart must have
stopped beating. The judge's deft fingers separated her
lips just long enough to ascertain that her teeth were in
proper alignment. Then the hands passed over her
neck and shoulders, down her rib cage, over hips and
hindquarters.

I kept my head low, my face averted.

With a swift practiced motion he reached beneath
her tail, lifted her hindquarters a few inches off the
ground, and dropped them. Kate's legs remained rigid
with fear; her feet landed not one millimeter from
where they had been.

Mr. Aberfeldy gave Kate's rump a quick pat and
said, "Well trained."

He moved toward the table that held his judging
book and the rows of ribbons. He marked the book. I
was sweating from every pore, and Kate was still
frozen in her terror.

Mr. Aberfeldy approached, paused dramatically,
then handed me the blue ribbon.

"Dandy little golden," he murmured.

The Blue Houdini

When Riff came along, I did not particularly want another dog. I was living in a tiny hillside cottage in a midwestern city then, working as a secretary during the day and writing books in the evenings and on weekends. Between these occupations and taking care of the house, a large yard, and Molly, my Bedlington terrier, there just didn't seem to be enough time to do justice to a second dog, especially of a breed that demanded so much grooming. I promised myself that in another year or two I could quit my job and move to the country to write. Then there would be time and space for all the dogs I wanted.

We got along well, Molly and I and our small calico cat, Valley. While I was at work, Molly and Valley napped in the house or went through the built-in dog door into the backyard, which was fenced for Molly's safety. For a terrier Molly was a low-strung individual. She didn't demand much exercise; she was content to spend the long evenings curled up on top of my feet while I sat at the typewriter. Valley usually chose to stretch her gaudy self along the desk top where she could bat at the jerking corner of the typing paper.

One evening a friend called from her home in a nearby town. She raised Bedlingtons—in fact, we had become acquainted through our common love for the lamblike dogs.

"I'm going nuts," she said for openers. "I've got a whole litter of pups, five months old, and not a single one of them sold yet. Could you take them, see if you can sell them for me on commission?"

The cottage had just been newly carpeted—I had rewrites to do on my new book within the next two weeks—I'd be away from home all day and unable to keep an eye on the pups. But on the other hand, five-month-old Bedlingtons; what a wealth of love and fun.

"I'll see what I can do. Bring them on down."

The next day they arrived, three gangly female pups and one male who was already noticeably larger than proper Bedlington size. It was soon obvious that none of them had ever been inside a house before. When the business arrangements were made and my friend had driven away, I sank into the davenport and wondered aloud what I had let myself in for.

The three girls were everywhere, noses down, tracking Molly and the cat, poking into every corner of the cottage. But the big male pup came directly to me. He shoved his bony chest against my knees and fixed his eyes on mine in the most penetrating stare I had ever felt. He was sending a message. I felt the impact of it.

He was a blue Bedlington, a color that in a poodle would be called silver but was actually a smoky blue-gray shading to white on head and legs. His coat was extremely dense, soft, woolly, unreal. Patting him was like pressing a roll of cotton batting. His head was long and lean, punctuated with a huge black nose and dark almond eyes. His ears were close-shaved, with luxuriant tassles on their tips. Given the rest of his body, he might have been a woolly greyhound, with deep flat rib cage, curved topline and shaved scimitar tail. He was going to be a good one, my hands told me as I went over him. Too big, but not coarse. Well-proportioned, powerful. Ideal for mating with the petite Molly.

No, no, Lynn, I cautioned myself. Use your common sense. Forget it. This coat would take half an hour a day to keep in good shape. You can't spare half an hour a day.

I tried to look away from him, to assess the bitch puppies so that I'd know how best to sell them. But the

big blue lamb stayed with me, forcing himself between me and whatever I was doing, keeping his
penetrating eyes fastened always on mine. It was
unnerving.

Later that night, when the other three were curled up
on the back porch, I got out Molly's pedigree and the
pup's, and sat down on the floor to study them. Molly
immediately worked her way under my elbow and
settled with a sigh, her head in my lap. It had been a
harrowing evening for her. The big pup heaved himself clumsily onto the davenport behind me and dropped a front paw over each of my shoulders. With his
head drooping down across my chest and one satin ear
pressed firmly against my cheek, he closed his eyes.

I whispered, "You big crazy mutt, you're the most
persistently love-starved dog I've ever seen. Even
among Bedlingtons you take the prize."

His tail quivered, and his head pressed more heavily
on my shoulder.

I unfolded his pedigree. Sire, Champion Center
Ridge Barbeedon. That explained the heavy coat, I
thought, and the ultra-sweet nature. His grandsire had
won Best in Show, all breeds, at Madison Square
Garden not many years before. The rest of his pedigree
was thick with champions and international champions.

You can't afford him, my better judgement warned.

Yes, but if I had him I wouldn't have to pay to have
Molly bred, I argued to myself. I'd be way ahead in the
long run.

You haven't the time to show him and campaign him right, and he's too big to get his championship without a lot of careful campaigning.

I know it. So I'll produce non-champion-sired pups. It's not all that important.

Better judgement shrugged and withdrew. It knew when it was beaten.

I got ready for bed, my mind searching for ways to scrape up the pup's price. Before I had pulled up the blankets, a large black nose bumped mine; a long white face came up over the edge of the bed and hesitated.

"Oh, all right, you might as well."

In a clumsy sprawling scramble he was up on the bed, shoving against me, settling his head on my shoulder so that he could continue his absurd hypnotic staring into my eyes.

I sighed. "I don't suppose you'd consider sleeping at the foot of the bed."

His tail lashed, and his long soft muzzle burrowed into my neck.

"For heaven's sake I give up. I'll buy you."

The next evening I called the pups' owner to tell her I wanted him. She said she had just received orders for two of the females that morning, and thought she might keep the third one herself. We laughed at the feast-or-famine puppy-selling business, and she said she'd be down to fetch the females home.

Choosing an official name for the pup was easy enough: Hope's Debonair of Hallmark. But from that I could derive no call name that suited him. The next afternoon I was driving home from work, singing, when suddenly I stopped to listen to myself. The music was "The Riffs' Theme," from the "Desert Song."

Riff. For reasons that had nothing to do with logic, the big blue pup looked like a Riff, and so that was it.

It was spring then, and I decided to take the next week off as part of my vacation. It would be good to have the time with Riff, to get him settled in his new home, and there was a great deal of work to be done around the cottage.

The vacation week was a small jewel. In the mornings I wrote, and in the afternoons Riff, Molly, Valley, and I were outdoors. I painted the trim on the white brick cottage, planted lilacs, and cleaned out the cellar while the dogs chased each other in circles that kept them always close to me. Now Riff was aiming his torrents of love at Molly, the cat, everyone he saw.

Saturday morning while I worked along the outside of the dog fence planting morning glories, I heard a child's voice whooping, "Yayhoo, Prince." I looked around to see the neighbors' huge old sorrel gelding trotting across the badminton court, head low, halter rope swaying, and three of his young owners bouncing on his back.

I grinned and waved at them. Prince was a neighborhood pet, almost a part of my own family. Often in the summer twilight I flung myself from the picnic table to the horse's broad bare back and loped around the block. When his owners went on vacation, I took care of him and pretended he was mine.

As the horse approached, Molly quietly slipped around the corner of the house. She had no liking for anything as high and bucket-footed as Prince. Valley kept her distance, too, in a more aloof manner, but Riff went to meet Prince, delighted at this new prospect.

I think someone once said, "A stranger is just a friend I haven't met yet." Nothing could have more precisely described Riff's creed.

At the dog's approach Prince stopped and lowered his head, ignoring the six small heels that drummed on his ribs. Riff's tail whipped the air as he bopped Prince's muzzle with his own. I don't know to what extent animals communicate with their nose-touching ceremonies, but for Riff this seemed to cement another love. Prince was unmoved.

The children soon tired of riding him, and tied the horse to the long rope that was anchored on the clothesline pole. He began to graze. Riff lay down as close as he could to the horse's constantly moving head.

"Riffy, get away from there," I called, afraid of Prince's hooves. He was a gentle animal and had been a town horse long enough not to be spooked by dogs, but still his hooves were so large, and Riff's plush body was so close beneath them, that I was unable to relax and go back to my planting.

Riff ignored my call. By this time I had learned one inescapable fact about my new dog. He was the most loving dog I had ever known, but he was simply not very smart.

His housebreaking had been relatively painless. After all, he was five months old and had constant access to the outdoors. But when I tried to teach him basic good manners such as "Come" and "Get down off of there" and "Don't jump up on people,"his mind became as fuzzy as his topknot. Stern tones broke his heart; no matter how gently I tried to show him what I wanted, he sensed disapproval and his mind went blank under torrents of shame and apology.

So I went to Riff and the horse, slapped Prince's neck in greeting, and led Riff into the house. It was lunchtime anyway.

While I began putting a quick lunch together under the cat's optimistic gaze, Riff and Molly banged through the dog door and out into the yard.

"That's fine," I murmured to the absent Riff. "You can admire Prince through the fence. You don't need to be right under his feet."

A few mintues later I heard Pat calling my name. She was the mother of Prince's young owners. I stuck my head out the back door.

"Looks as though Riffy likes old Prince," she said around a mouthful of clothespins. Her hands were full of wind-whipped sheets, but she motioned with her head toward Riff, who was once again curled up within a foot of the horse's grass-tearing teeth. Although Molly didn't like Prince, she was running back and forth along the fence, jealous of Riff's freedom.

Quickly I checked the gate. It was closed and latched. The fence was four feet high, of sturdy woven wire. Although it was by no means maximum security, it had always held Molly and the occasional dogs who came for trimming. It had never occurred to me to distrust the fence.

Again I retrieved my cotton-coated horse lover and deposited him with something less than tenderness within the confines of the fence. Most of the afternoon I spent watching Riff, catching him time after time in the act of climbing over the fence. Each time I scolded more harshly and slapped his hip more sharply. He was increasingly sorry about the whole thing but not sorry enough to abandon his attempts. It wasn't until Pat and I finally led Prince to his pasture, out of sight beyond my orchard, that Riff gave up his escape attempts and turned his attention back to me.

On Monday morning, as I was trying to settle myself into the office routine after my week of freedom, the phone rang.

"Lynn? This is Pat. Listen, Riff is out. He went over the fence just as you were driving away, and he took off after your car. I tried to find him, and just couldn't. I thought I'd better let you know, though."

I thought of the heavy Monday morning rush-hour traffic, the country-raised pup trying to follow my car.

"You're sure he's not in the pasture with Prince?" I said, hoping for the least dangerous possibility.

"No, I looked."

I thanked her and hung up. Ours was a very small office, just my boss and me, and luckily he was a dog lover also. I told him what had happened.

"What did you have to do today?" he asked.

"Just write those four commercials for the bank."

He waved me away. "I'll do those. You go look for your pooch."

I drove the forty blocks to the cottage as slowly as possible, searching the street and curbs for a gray mound of dog body. I stared at the passing sidewalks and front yards, hoping to see him. When I got home, only Molly and Valley were there. Prince's pasture held only Prince. I searched all afternoon, trying not to think about the rumors of dog thieves.

Finally, when I could think of nothing else to try, I called the Animal Shelter and asked if the dogcatchers had brought in a Bedlington terrier.

"I don't know," the voice said. "We got a funny-looking gray poodle this afternoon, though."

The poodle was indeed Riff. His joy was so frenzied that I was barely able to pay the fifteen-dollar fine to bail him out. His voice was a high, nearly human keening; he flung himself time after time at my chest; he fairly cried with relief.

So did I. On the way home I said, "I hope you've learned your lesson, you big crazy teddy bear. Now do you see why I tried to make you stay inside the fence?"

With nose and patting paws he swore obedience to the fence.

The next afternoon Pat called to say that Riff was out again. On my way home from work I stopped at the Shelter, paid another fifteen-dollar fine, and took home my delighted blue lamb.

It was obvious that the fence was no more than an inconvenience to Riff. It was equally obvious that I could not afford to continue paying his fines even if I was willing to let him take his chances running loose, which I wasn't.

To add to the problem on that second day of Riff's defection we returned home to find Molly huddled on the front doorstep. It appeared that she, who had never before thought of climbing the fence, had learned to do so under Riff's influence but then had had the sense to stay home.

After much sighing and refiguring of my budget I called the lumberyard and ordered a five-foot chain link fence, to be professionally installed as soon as possible around the dog yard. The price was nearly five-hundred dollars, but it would be worth it, I rationalized, if it would keep the dogs in and safe.

The fence could not be installed for several days, however, so the next morning, with regret especially for Molly, who was not to blame, I locked both dogs inside the house with newspapers on the back porch floor.

When I came home that afternoon, the house was in order, nothing had been chewed or destroyed, the newspapers had been properly used. But on one arm of the davenport and all around the dust ruffle of the bed were streaks of urine. Riff was, of course, wildly happy to see me.

"Did you do that?" I asked in theatrical tones of disgust, showing him the streaks. "Aren't you *ashamed?*"

Yes. He was utterly ashamed, and he promised on his back never to do it again.

I got through the days that followed by covering as much of the furniture as possible with old plastic tablecloths and dry-cleaner bags before I left for work, and mopping up with appropriate disgust when I came home. I prayed for the fence installers.

At long last they came. They were just finishing the stretching and clamping when I arrived home in the late afternoon. Five-hundred dollars worth of lovely chain link fence stretched around the back yard as high as my head, Riff-proof. With great relief and a feeling of conquest I unlocked the dog door and let Molly and Riff out into their yard.

The installers began to load their tools into the truck. I stood nearby, enjoying the sight of my two free and happy dogs.

"What kind of dogs are them, anyhow?" one of the men asked.

"Bedlington terriers. It's an English breed."

"Funny-looking things. Look like sheep to me," he muttered good-naturedly.

I smiled, thinking of the prices Molly's pups would bring this winter.

The men slammed the truck doors, waved, and drove away. Still smiling, I turned around just in time to see Riff teetering awkwardly on the top of the new fence. With a final thrust he half jumped, half fell to freedom and came to me in a rush of pride and love. It was difficult, that first climb over a fence so high, and he wanted appreciation.

Riff developed into a mature dog who was, in his way, magnificent, if such an adjective can be applied to an animated plush toy of a dog.

But his escapist tendencies persisted. His fascination for Prince cooled somewhat, so he seldom climbed the fence for any reason except to get to me. If I left him in the house and ran next door for a few minutes, Riff was, almost immediately, scratching at Pat's back door with an expression that seemed to say, "Is Lynn in there? She forgot to take me."

Leaving for work in the morning still held an element of battle. At first, after the new fence proved worthless, I simply turned the lock screw on the swinging dog door, confining both dogs in the house. Within three days Riff devised a way of shoving against one edge of the door panel until the other side slipped past the lock screw. Again he was delighted to

see me when I came to the Animal Shelter to pay his
fine and bail him out.

Then I tried hooking the door between the kitchen
and the back porch, where the dog door was. Riff met
the challenge of the latch, and once again the Animal
Shelter was richer for his visit. I began to suspect they
kept a dogcatcher's wagon permanently posted in my
neighborhood.

Everyone I talked to had a solution for the problem.

"Electric fence," my boss said.

Electric fences were forbidden within the city lim-
its.

"Run a strip of chicken wire around the top of the
fence, slanting in," a friend said.

I tried it. Riff was only temporarily inconvenienced
and had to revise his climbing techniques.

"Tie him up," another friend said. I shook my head,
envisioning Riff getting loose, climbing the fence with
a length of chain dragging behind, possibly hanging
himself.

"Get rid of the damn dog."

"No, Dad," I said, "I'll work something out."

Eventually I invented a system of locks that was
Riff-proof, but even then, at least once a month when
the meter reader came, Riff managed to get out, to get
himself picked up, and to require fine money. He came
to be a familiar boarder at the Shelter, and he helped a
great deal with their operating expenses. I was a
grudging fixture about the place myself, and I always

had the feeling that behind my back the employees were jeering at anyone who would pay three times the value of her dog in fines. One kennelman in particular seemed to sneer. He was a pock-faced young man whose insolence was only barely hidden.

"One of these days I'm going to leave you with that man," I told Riff every time I drove him home. It was an empty threat, of course, but the fines were making serious inroads into my salary and I could see no end to it.

As the months passed, Riff grew somewhat resigned to my leaving him during the day. He still protested by anointing the davenport daily, and he still could not be trusted outdoors in my absence, but we managed a more or less peaceful existence.

It was my infrequent absences during the evening that he most resented. During these times he managed an incredible amount of squirting, on kitchen cupboards, stove and refrigerator, or bookcases and bedspreads. It had nothing to do with housebreaking; I understood that now. It was a deliberate act, born either of insecurity or spite.

One night in November I left for my weekly evening at the laundromat. In my struggle with the basket of clothes, the box of detergent, and a book to read, I apparently failed to pull the door completely shut. When I came back an hour later, the front door stood open six inches and Riff was gone. Molly waited inside, trembling.

I drafted the neighbor children, the oldest of whom now had a driver's license, and we set out in our two cars to comb the neighborhood. No Riff.

I went to bed thinking it would serve him right to spend the night at the Shelter. But when I called for him the following day, he wasn't there. Hadn't been picked up. I left both my home and office phone numbers and asked to be called as soon as Riff was brought in.

No call came. The days went by, and became weeks and finally months. At first I was frantic, and then just heartsore. Forgotten were the fines, the battle to keep the cottage free from the smell of urine. Everything I tried to write turned sour.

When he had been gone for five months, I began reluctantly to think about finding another mate for Molly. A daughter from the first mating of Molly and Riff was now a well-known champion making a name for herself on the Florida show circuits, and I was beginning to get requests for pups from the same breeding.

It would be impossible, I felt, to find another dog whose genes meshed so ideally with Molly's, and of course no other dog could fill the very special Riff-shaped hole in my life. But I began a desultory search anyhow.

One spring Sunday the local paper carried an ad that read, "Bedlington terrier male, 6 mos, no papers, $30."

At first I felt little interest. A dog that couldn't be

registered would be useless for breeding, and I knew how few supposedly purebred dogs that are offered "without papers" are actually purebred. And thirty dollars was about a fifth the going rate for Bedlingtons, so it couldn't be much of a dog.

Still, there were so few of the breed in town, in fact in the entire state, that my curiosity was finally piqued. I began to wonder if this pup might show a trait of coat or ear carriage or build that would tell me his bloodline.

What the heck, I thought. I'll just take a ride over and have a look at him.

The address in the ad was one of the poorer parts of the city, big ugly old houses made over into smelly ocher-colored apartments. I rang the bell at one of them.

From inside came the sound of furiously barking dogs. The man who admitted me was as unappetizing to look at as I had expected, considering the surroundings. Although I was sure we had never met, something about his long, carelessly shaven face was familiar. I told him I wanted to see the Bedlington terrier.

The room in which we stood was uncarpeted and almost bare of furniture but crowded with dog crates and pens of every size, all of them occupied. The stench was nearly unbreatheable.

When I told him what I wanted, the man's face became animated. "Oh sure. This here is a real good dog. It's a thoroughbred, but see, his papers got lost here a while back, so he ain't registered or nothing. But he's a real good dog."

"Let's see him," I said drily.

At the sound of my voice a sudden high keening came from one of the crates. The man opened this crate, and out shot a large, incredibly filthy yellowish dog with an unBedlingtonlike round head, long legs that were nearly bare of coat, a tail from which were suspended chunks of matted filth. The hair on his ears, feet, and parts of his neck grew in wiry black patches.

While I was mentally reeling from the looks of the animal, he flung himself at my chest, whining, crying, barking, scattering my rope of beads in all directions, driving his muzzle into my ear. My arms went around him, stink and all, and I wet his neck with my tears.

"I think he likes you, lady," the man said, grinning in anticipation of an easy sale.

I answered indignantly, "I should hope to kiss a pregnant duck. This dog belongs to me, and I have the registration at home to prove it. How did you ever get your hands on him?"

I didn't know whether to be furious or frightened. This was, after all, no neighborhood in which a woman alone should start an argument.

The man's expression became guarded. "You might have some kind of registration for a Bedlington terrier, lady, but that ain't no proof that it's for this dog. This one is just a puppy, just six months old. See, all Bedlingtons are born black, and he ain't even lost all of his puppy coat yet. That's how you can tell how old he is."

For the first time in my life I used a genuinely vulgar expression aloud. "This dog is three years old. They don't lose their puppy coats in splotches like that, for heaven's sake. He's been injured. Any time a blue Bedlington's skin is broken the hair grows in black. I'm taking him out of here, and if you try to stop me, I'll have every policeman in town down here checking you out."

Shaking with fear and fury, I turned and stalked down the hall with Riff in my arms. I was braced for a running tackle, a blow on the back of the head, television-style, at least an angry shout from the man. Nothing happened. I got out of the building, into the car, and away.

As soon as we were safely away from the area, I pulled over to the curb and, with trembling hands, examined Riff carefully. His ears were badly infected from all those months of not being cleaned. Beneath the mats he was shockingly thin and covered with small scars, but otherwise he seemed none the worse for whatever experiences the past five months had brought him. The roundness of his head was all wool and would be corrected with clippers and scissors; the rest of his formerly luxurious coat would have to be shaved off at the skin, it was so solidly matted. The black spots would grow out and disappear, and eventually he would be his old gorgeous self.

And somehow I knew that he had learned his lesson now. After what he must have gone through, he was never going to climb over that fence again. It would be just a few months now before the long-dreamed-of house in the country would be a reality. All Riff had to do was refrain from escaping until then, and we'd be home free.

Suddenly I realized whom his captor had reminded me of—the surly kennel man at the Animal Shelter. If they were related... I determined to call the authorities as soon as I got home.

When we reached the cottage, Riff tore around and around the yard, his tail ruddering around the corners, his voice crying out his joy. He went through the cottage, sweeping up Molly, racing out into the dog yard with Molly in close pursuit.

I watched for a few moments, then ran next door to spread the good news. While I waited at the back door for my knock to be answered, I turned to savor the sight of my miraculously returned favorite.

He was teetering on the fence top, striving to escape and come to me.

The Quick Black Fox

1

Maggie came to Touchwood under a burden of expectancy and prejudice too great for any pup. She was bought as a replacement for Megan, and although I willed her to be a second Megan, I expected, even before her arrival, to be disappointed.

Perhaps if Megan had lived longer than six months I would have become inured to her perfection, or the perfection would have shown itself to be flawed. Instead, her life ended with a playful pass at a friend's car in the lane behind the house, while she was still new enough to be a source of wonder. She had given every promise of being the once-in-a-lifetime dog that every breeder dreams of.

Megan was my first border collie. I had studied the breed at length before deciding on the bloodline I wanted; then I waited four months for the litter to arrive. Finally I studied the entire litter with almost fanatic intensity before making my choice; I was buying not only a dog but the beginning of my own kennel, the Touchwood bloodline.

Most of the studying was needless, though. Meg was the first pup to catch my eye, and the only one I seriously considered after that first look. I saw nothing but perfection in her markings, her bone structure, her movements. Even at six weeks of age she carried herself smartly, head high, tiny tail low but upcurved at the tip. Her puppy fur was a dense velvet black edged in white on feet, tail tip, and chest, and in a narrow blaze down her face.

Her round eyes stared directly into mine with an expression neither fatuous nor fearful. When I sat on the floor of her kennel, she climbed across my legs and flattened herself upward against my chest because she had chosen to like me, not because of automatic competition with the other pups. Even at that age she was a thinker.

On the four-hour drive back to Touchwood she lay beside me on the car seat, head up, fearlessly interested in the sound and smell of the car heater, the motion of my hand on the steering wheel, the glinting sunlight on the dashboard. When my hand had time to come down to her, she was happy; otherwise she was content.

From her first moments at Touchwood Megan carried herself with aplomb. Nothing intimidated her, not the boisterous welcome of Riff, my only remaining Bedlington terrier, nor the strangeness of the house itself. She spent her first night alone in the pantry with only a pile of my old sweatshirts for company, and made no sound of complaint. Although she was just six weeks old, she had her bladder under control; there were no nighttime failures. In four days she was housebroken. Any accidents that occurred after that were caused by my failure to see her at the door.

It was winter then, and Touchwood stood at the mercy of the winds, but Megan was soon leading me on long cold explorations of barn and orchard. She reveled in snowdrifts and relished the push of the wind.

Touchwood was a farmhouse, unpretentious for northeast Iowa but with an honest sort of grace. It was more than a century old, thick-walled, brick, rotting here and there around its porches, and beset with plumbing eccentricities, yet it remained solid, calm, comfortable. The farm was small, flat and devoted entirely to corn, which grew up close around the house yard. Mammoth windbreak pines, as old as the house or older, sheltered it from the wind and from the eyes of the town beyond the fields.

The deep wishes of childhood hold truths of our

natures that are seldom found in adult goals. Touchwood was, for me, the fruition of a plan begun as far
back as my earliest memories. It was freedom and
solitude; it was mine, bought and sustained by my
labor. And Megan was an inextricable part of that plan.
She was to be the foundation on which the Touchwood Kennel would be built. In every way she was a
thoroughbred, but of a breed only a few people knew
well enough to appreciate, and to me this was an added
value.

As soon as spring released us, Megan, Riff, and I
began taking long walks, over the hump of a neighbor's oat field and into the woods beyond.

It was a large rambling timber, spreading for miles
up the juttings of stream valleys. Huge trees that had
grown themselves to death lay along the ground under
vine blankets, the pillars of their branches making
shelters for rabbits and children from town who came
there to play forbidden games. In the spring women
hiked into the woods in twos and threes, wearing old
jackets and scarves to keep the ticks off. If they were
lucky, they filled their sacks with spongelike mush-
rooms. If not, they went home exhilarated by the forest
darkness. In the fall a few boys and old men came to
hunt the valuable ginseng roots. But the woods were
large enough so that even at these busy times the dogs
and I seldom saw anyone.

In the oat field Megan would make sweeping runs
before me, but always with one eye on me. A wave of

my arm sent her in the indicated direction or brought her back to me, although she had not as yet had training of any kind. Riff, meanwhile, was off on uncontrolled races with birds or squirrels.

At six months Megan was a handsome sight. She was nearly collie-size and built like the collies of the pre-dog-show era, a glossy blue-black animal whose carriage and symmetry were a mobile pedigree. Her coat was long, nearly straight, dense and silky to the touch.

By this time she had mastered all of the commands for novice obedience competition, even though the training sessions, ten minutes a day, had begun just two weeks before. Meg reveled in her accomplishments. At the sight of the training collar and leash she ran to the front yard and sat herself precisely, tensely, trying not to wag her tail until I caught up with her. A new exercise need only be shown to her a few times; then she caught on and delighted in performing it over and over. Her eyes never left mine; she drew approval from me with the intensity of her desire to win it.

And then she was dead.

A neighbor took the shining dog away and buried her with his own pets in an old hollyhock garden.

Some people say, at the loss of a loved pet, that they could not think of replacing the dead one with another. For me the only surcease is to fill the hole as quickly as possible with a new personality. Before I was even able to speak coherently, I called Megan's breeder and put my name on the waiting list for another pup from the same sire and dam. Fortunately the breeding had been repeated, and the new litter, now two weeks old, still had one available female pup.

During the month before she was old enough to bring home, I had ample time to build expectations of the unseen pup, and the expectations followed exactly the lines of Megan's accomplishments.

The days moved past with summer slowness. I wrote. I tore out the rusted tangles of barbed-wire fence that sagged from rotten posts at the edge of the backyard. I rode with Karen, a young friend whose horse was in summer residence in Touchwood's huge red stone-based barn.

My nearest neighbor was a widower, a retired farmer and incurable horseman. Although he was eighty that year, he owned a spirited young horse and rode her daily. Star was a small fine mare, half Arab, half Morgan, a pleasing blend of the good qualities of both breeds. She was thin-skinned and long of pastern, and her coat was a black that did not fade to brown in the summer. Because I was so fond of the little mare, her owner, Roy, encouraged me to borrow her.

During those time-marking days Star and I, Karen and her big bay, Sunup, circled the fields and penetrated the woods. We practiced cantering in figure-eights on the town baseball diamond. We took sacks of sandwiches and rode across the highway and through a smaller wood to a steep-walled secret valley where an abandoned stone mill waited in the sun. We tied the horses and explored the mill, climbing from floor to floor and walking cautiously on suspect boards.

In these pleasant ways the month passed and the new pup was old enough to bring home.

2

The drive home from the kennel seemed to take forever. The afternoon was hot. My fingers stuck to each other, and my legs stuck to the car seat.

"This is the last car I buy without air conditioning," I muttered to the pup beside me.

Throughout the month of waiting for this dog I had been aware of the intensity of my anticipation, and I was braced for a disappointment. Maggie was a disappointment. The bracing for it did not help.

I glanced down at her as I drove with one hand and tried to drink a bottle of pop with the other. The pup had been crying constantly, and struggling to climb my arm.

There had been only three female pups from which to choose, and although this one appeared to be the best of the three, she fell dismally short of Megan's perfection. She carried herself nicely, and she was well enough put together, but her extreme nervousness in the car worried me. This pup, like Megan, was to be the foundation for the Touchwood bloodline, and one quality I wanted most to avoid was a nervous, timid temperament.

Besides, I didn't like her markings. Instead of the

narrow white blaze down her face that had set off
Megan's expression so smartly, this pup had a large
white spot, roughly heart-shaped, which covered most
of her forehead from ears to eyes and trickled down
between her eyes to become a white muzzle. Instead of
the full white collar I'd hoped for, she had just a
diamond-shaped spot on the back of her neck. These
were not unusual markings for a border collie, but the
white forehead gave her whole head a large, coarse,
staring look, an unattractive expression.

I had previously decided to register her as Touchwood's Megan, and later I did so, but now, driving
home with her, I found that something in me balked at
calling her Megan. I resented her for falling short of
the name. She became Maggie.

When at last we got home, I put her in the newly
fenced dog yard, built after Megan's death to insure
the safety of this new pup. I longed for the cool rooms
inside the house, and for a bath to remove the sticky
spilled pop on my shin, but I sat down for a few
minutes to watch Maggie. She met Riff's welcoming
charge stolidly, allowing him to sniff her over; then
she sank her teeth into his bony tail.

Good, I thought, at least she's not timid with him.

I went into the kitchen, did a quick mop-job on my
shin, then stood at the window watching the two dogs.
Touchwood's kitchen was a long room, formerly a
porch, across the back of the house. In the far end was
a door leading to the caricature of a woodshed, beyond

which was the dog yard. Recently a small swinging dog door had been built into the bottom of the door from kitchen to woodshed, so that the dogs could go from house to fenced yard at will, rather than waking me during the night each time they wanted to go out and bark at owls.

After a few moments Riff came banging through the dog door to finish welcoming me home. I ruffled his woolly topknot, thinking that I should probably go out and bring in the pup. But before I had worked myself up to leaving the blessed coolness of the house, the flap of the dog door moved tentatively inward. It must be the wind, I thought. Surely that little bit of a pup . . .

But one tiny black leg appeared through the door. Then a muzzle, a bright dark eye, a white heart. With incredible clumsiness the puppy tumbled through the door. I watched in disbelief. The bottom of the dog door was as high as Maggie's back, and she not only had to push it open but to hold out the door and its loose, windbreaking rim while she hauled her fat self up, over, and through the opening. It had taken days of patient work to teach Riff to use the door, and he was a grown dog.

I picked up the puppy. "By golly, we've got to give you points for brains and guts, anyway."

For a while I felt better about her prospects, but that night she cried endlessly and would not be left alone. Any pup in strange surroundings might have done the same, but I couldn't help thinking of Megan's calm, intelligent acceptance of new things.

Oddly enough, after that first night Maggie began to show a strong spirit of independence. She chose to sleep alone in the woodshed, and most of her waking hours were spent playing by herself in the yard. She enjoyed falling, scraping, banging through the dog door, and often went in and out, in and out, just to amuse herself.

One afternoon when she was about three months old I started up the lane to visit Roy and Star, with Maggie along for company. Roy had not seen her yet, and I thought the walk might be fun for the pup.

The lane to Touchwood was perhaps the length of two city blocks, and before its final approach to the house it curved sharply north. It was a very narrow dirt track with corn growing so close beside it that during the fall, hard ears of corn would strike the sides of the car. It was late summer now, and walking in the curved lane was much like exploring a jungle, the cornstalks grew so thick and close and towered so high over my head. I loved the almost-lost feeling of it.

We started out, with Maggie darting ahead to attack a cloud of small yellow moths that shimmered over a mud puddle in the lane. Suddenly, while my attention wandered, she vanished.

"Maggie," I called. She did not appear. I listened for a rustling in the corn, but heard nothing. "Maggie, come out of there. NOW."

I called, commanded, searched and thrashed up and down the narrow corn rows while the sharp leaf-edges cut at my bare arms and legs. I sweated and swore and called. When at length I gave up and fought my way back to the lane, Maggie was sitting in the exact middle of the track watching me, tense with the fun of eluding me.

We went on to Roy's house with Maggie leashed. The old gentleman was sitting on his front porch, listening to his radio and waving at passing cars. His was the last house on the last street of town, but on this mild September evening many people were out in their cars, couples taking elderly relatives for a slow spin around town, teen-agers using the family car to escape home and parents for a few hours. Everyone knew Roy and waved as they went by.

I left Maggie in Roy's company and went around to the barn to see Star. She had been bred to an Arabian stallion a few months before, and I was eager to see the first sign of an enlarged abdomen.

When I came back, the man and the pup had cemented a friendship. Maggie was on his lap, propped away from him with one stiff foreleg against his chest, and staring into his face while he talked to her.

"That's funny," I said. "She's never been a lap dog at all, with me."

"She's a good old pup," Roy said, talking into Maggie's face.

"Yes. Well, we'd better be getting home. I meant to

stay longer, but I spent most of the evening chasing Good Old Pup through the accursed cornfield."

When we got home, I sat down on the living room floor and called Maggie to me. She came, and for a minute she stayed, but then she pulled away and left on business of her own. I looked after her, puzzled and foolishly hurt.

All through her puppyhood Maggie was, with me, a noncuddler. She came when I called her, but after touching base she was off again. In the evenings when the fire was lit and the television on, she should have come to curl up against me as Riff did, but she was busy in the yard or asleep alone in the woodshed. With Roy, with any stranger who came to the door, she was as affectionate as a puppy could be. But never with me.

In October another pup was added to the family, a chunky, well-bred, and beautifully marked border collie named Touchwood Lad. From the first Lad was a dedicated body-contact dog. When I walked, he strived to remain pressed against my left ankle. When I sat, he was immediately across my foot or, if possible, my lap. After his arrival I paid less attention to Maggie's haughtiness.

Maggie accepted Lad as another toy provided for her amusement. She quit demolishing Riff and turned her energies to buffeting and chewing the new pup. Yet there seemed to be in her actions no trace of the jealousy that might have been expected.

Often I took both pups outdoors with Riff and me

while I worked in the garden, which was at the front of the house near the lane. I was spading it up in preparation for next year's seed, and putting winter mulch around the rose and raspberry bushes. Lad never wandered farther than the length of the laces of my tennis shoes, but Maggie watched until my attention was on something other than her; then, with care and craftiness, she melted into the cornfield. I would go to the edge of the field and command her to come out. Eventually, when my patience was all but gone, I'd hear a noise behind me and Maggie would be there, having circled the house and barns under cover of the corn and approached from the opposite direction.

As she matured, the objectionable white spot on Maggie's head seemed to grow smaller and longer in proportion to the rest of her head. Perhaps it was simply that her skull lengthened more than it broadened, and drew the marking out with it. At any rate it occurred to me one day that I rather liked the spot. The coat that replaced her puppy fuzz was longer and thicker than Megan's had been, and more curly. I began to see Maggie as a potentially good looking dog. Her ear carriage, which is often problematical in collie breeds, was perfect—erect except for the top third of the ears, which fell softly forward.

Then, when she was less than five months old, she stopped growing. She was just under seventeen inches at that time. As her coat became longer, she took on the appearance of a short-legged dog although beneath her coat her body was correctly proportioned, no longer than it was high. To add to my dismay, her left ear began to stand fully erect. Now she looked not only squatty but lopsided, with one ear upright and the other tipped forward.

Within a few weeks, though, the second ear joined the first. Maggie was now a prick-eared border collie. Prick ears are perfectly acceptable in the border collie breed. Many fine dogs have them, and many breeders like them. But I did not. Megan's ears had not been upright.

By now Maggie was more fox than collie in appearance, and perhaps in character. Her body seemed low and long although it wasn't; her tail was a great thick brush; her face beneath the small pointed ears was similarly small and pointed. Her skull was a shade too short and round, her muzzle a shade too snipy. And her eyes held a constant underglow of challenge.

In November, when she was six months old, I began giving her short obedience lessons in the afternoons when I had finished writing. We worked in the front yard, while Lad and Riff watched through the windows. It was a relaxation for me, after hours at the typewriter, and I was curious to compare Maggie's learning ability with Megan's. I had no plans to show Maggie—I was not even sure I was going to keep her—but I wanted to make the comparison.

For several days the lessons were fast and smooth. Behind her pert face Maggie's mind was sharp and eager for exercise. She absorbed each new command almost as fast as I could show her what it was that I wanted her to do. When she did something well, I made a great fuss over her, hugging her and telling her she was wonderful. It was standard training procedure, done with little personal meaning on my part, but her reaction to my praise was surprising. She seemed hungry for it—Maggie, the embodiment of independence.

Unconsciously I began pushing her, introducing new commands faster than I ordinarily would have done, going over and over the old ones, insisting that every "sit" be square and every "stay" motionless. The more I pushed, the harder she tried, and the more edgy I became. The dog was doing amazingly well, and yet I came away from each session feeling irrationally snappy.

Inevitably, one afternoon, she rebelled. It had been the sort of day in which I should not have attempted to train her at all. After working for several weeks on a new book I had realized, just that morning, that the book was no good. It had been alive and now it was dead, and I wasn't sure why. Besides, it was a cold, cloudy winter-tasting day, and I dreaded the problems of winter at Touchwood. And I had a canker sore.

I took Maggie out to the front yard anyway, and we began.

"Heel."

We set off down the walk, around the pines, between

the rosebush and the strawberry bed. The wind hurt
the rims of my ears, and Maggie dragged along one
pace behind me. She had never done that before.

"Heel!"

She corrected herself, but when I turned right, she
cut across behind me and came up on the wrong side.

I halted and said, "Stand."

She lay down. In her eyes defiance burned.

With barely controlled patience I reached under her
and propped her into a standing position. Her legs
remained rigid, but her head and tail were as close to
the ground as she could make them.

I felt a boiling anger that came very close to hatred,
but I felt something else, too, a vengeful lacing of joy. I
wanted to hit her. I didn't do it, but I wanted to.

Suddenly her head came up. Her face turned toward
the lane, and her tail began to move. Star was trotting
toward us, with Roy hunched on her back.

"Okay, Maggie, lesson's over. Good girl." With a
sense of escaped disaster I released her.

Roy brought Star up beside me. "You don't ever
come to visit a feller anymore, so Star and me thought
we'd come visit you."

He dismounted and received into his arms the
delighted Maggie. She leaped and licked and lashed
herself at him in a fury of love such as she had never
shown to me.

"Hey, Roy, how would you trade me, a horse for a
dog?" I took Star's reins.

He just laughed. "Go on, take her for a ride. She

needs the exercise, her and that little colt she's carrying. Maggie and I will just sit here and keep each other company." He lowered himself to the front steps and bent his head to meet Maggie's.

As I rode, the tension began to ease away. Sunup had been sold a few months before, when Karen began her senior year in high school, and I had done almost no riding since then. I'd forgotten the therapeutic effect of Star's singlefoot gait. She was in winter coat now, and furry as a pony, but she was still pretty enough to make me feel better just looking ahead between her stiff little ears.

I rode as long as I dared and came back feeling better, but I could not quite forget that moment of hate, and the corresponding pleasure I'd felt in the hating. I disliked myself and, unfairly, I disliked Maggie for exposing my ugliness.

3

A few nights later I received a phone call from a breeder and importer of border collies. I had written to him describing the kind of dog I was hoping to buy, the kind that Maggie had failed to become.

"I may have one you'd like," the man said. "She's a Scottish import I just had shipped over, a two-year-old bitch, trained for sheepdog trials. She's a big good-looking dog with semipricked ears, a narrow blaze on her face and a full white collar like you wanted. Her sire is an international champion, one of the top dogs in Scotland." I was duly impressed by the name of the dog, and he went on. "She's a sweet dog, very affectionate. I think you'd like her."

I said, "How soon can you put her on a plane?"

Three days later Lass arrived. It was late at night when her plane was due in, and our tiny airport was all but closed. I had spent the last hour in the baggage room drinking coffee, playing cards with the three men who were still on duty, and watching for the lights of the plane.

Don't get your hopes up, I warned myself over and over while I waited. Don't build up another disappointment like Maggie.

The plane coasted in. I stood down from the desk on which I'd been sitting and began nervously unrolling the lead in my pocket. My hour-long friend, the baggage man, wheeled in the wagon on which sat the large wooden crate that held my hopes.

We lifted down the crate. While I worked at the catch, I said, foolishly, "Lass? I'm your new mother." A tail thumped the walls of the crate. The door came open and out snaked Lass.

I sighed and relaxed. No disappointments this time. She was as advertised. Although she was thin and dull of coat from the ordeal of thousands of miles of travel, the important things were there—the conformation, the ears and markings, and love. She wrapped herself around me and lashed her tail so furiously that she bent in mid-spine with every wag.

On the long drive home Lass lay with her head across my lap, her tail moving with every word I spoke to her. For the first time I began thinking seriously of selling Maggie. This dog was what I wanted Touchwood border collies to be, not squatty prick-eared combatants.

It was late and cold when we got back to Touchwood. I put Lass in the seldom-used kennel, brought her huge quantities of food and water, which she gulped down; then I went inside to bed.

The next morning I brought her into the house and introduced her to the other dogs. Riff and Lad were predictably happy about her; Maggie looked her over briefly, then banged out through the dog door. I could hear her in the woodshed tossing chunks of firewood into the air. It was a sport she and Lad had invented as soon as the winter's supply of wood was put in the shed.

I spent most of the morning with Lass, showing her how to work the dog door, brushing the dullness out of her black coat, telling her I hoped she wasn't homesick for Scotland. She responded with adoration.

After lunch the usual procedure was for all the dogs to curl up on the couch in the den while I worked at my desk there throughout the afternoon. Today Lad and Riff took their accustomed corners of the couch, and Lass stretched out against the legs of my chair. But Maggie was stubbornly absent.

I tried to concentrate on the work in front of me, but

it didn't seem right to ignore Maggie's absence. Finally I went out to the woodshed door and opened it. Maggie was curled into a shivering knot on the cold concrete of the shed floor.

"Come on in where it's warm," I said.

She stared up at me with unblinking eyes.

"Or else stay out there. I *will* be obeyed." There was a note of laughter in my voice. If Maggie wanted to be petulant, it was all right with me. I had work to do.

At suppertime Maggie was still in the shed. Knowing that she could hear every sound that was made in the kitchen, I began loudly picking up dog dishes, scooping meal into them, adding water and canned food and bacon fat with unnecessarily loud scraping.

"Sure smells good," I told the other dogs in a carrying voice.

No response from the woodshed.

I set down the dishes with an unmistakable sound of plastic bowls against linoleum.

"I guess Lass is going to have to eat Maggie's too," I announced.

The dog door banged, but Maggie did not come through it. It was a metal door, which, when swung inward, struck a movable metal rim designed to keep out drafts. It was well-built but noisy.

"Come on in, Maggie, my love," I urged.

Bang-bang-bang-bang-bang. Maggie struck at the door several times in quick succession but did not come through.

"Oh, don't be silly," I said. "You've been operating that door since you were six weeks old. Get in here and eat your supper."

BANG-BANG-BANG-BANG-BANG.

I went to the door, suddenly afraid that she was hurt and unable to get through the dog door. I opened it and looked out.

Maggie sat just outside, waiting pertly. Something in her eyes made me feel that I had been manipulated. She rose, came wagging and smiling into the house, pressed herself against my legs for a moment, then dove at her food.

The next weekend I bought two middle-aged sheep from a boy in a neighboring town. They had been part of a Four-H project he had started a few years before, but now he was preparing for college and was cutting down the size of his flock. The sheep, whom I named Mary and Mary because at first I could not tell them apart, were both due to lamb in a few months. I told myself I wanted them because Lass had been trained for sheepherding competition and it would be a shame to let her forget what she had been taught. Also, now that Sunup was gone, the small orchard pasture would grow to weeds without something to graze it down. The truth was that I wanted them because sheep had always seemed such appealing animals, and the lambs would be fun to watch.

As soon as Mary and Mary had had a few days to get used to their new home, I tried Lass out. A set of instructions had come with her, the proper commands to make her move left and right, farther out or closer in, to gather the sheep, hold them, move them. I had watched other border collie handlers work their dogs, and I was eager to try my hand, and Lass's.

She followed me into the orchard, half crouched and trembling with anticipation at the sight and smell of the sheep. Mary and Mary stood twenty or thirty feet away, watching and chewing. I glanced at the paper on which I had jotted the commands.

"Okay, girl, here we go," I breathed. Then, firmly, "Lass, come by."

According to the directions this meant that she should go out around the sheep in a clockwise direction and approach them from the rear. She started toward them, creeping, staring at them with a fixed eye. But she didn't go out around. She crept a few steps, then turned to look back at me.

"Come by," I repeated, motioning toward the two ewes who were still watching with bland curiosity.

Again Lass moved a little closer, but she seemed confused. Mary and Mary turned their backs to us and went back to their grazing.

I decided to try counterclockwise. With another glance at the direction sheet I said, "Lass, go 'way to me!" and motioned in the direction she was to go.

She moved hesitantly to the right, then turned once again and stared back at me, head cocked, eyes pleading for clarification.

Suddenly I laughed. "I bet I know what's the matter, old Lassie." In my best late-movie Scottish brogue I said, "All richt noo, my gurrrrl. Awa' ye go. Loss, coom byie!"

Her ears flicked back against her head. Surely and smoothly she veered to the left, circled the flock of two, and, with a series of masterful crouches and dashes, pushed the ewes toward me.

We worked for half an hour, herding the sheep around and among the ancient apple trees until the Marys became cranky and began butting at Lass when she tried to drive them.

"Okay, Lass, that's enough for today. We'll do some more tomorrow."

With extreme reluctance Lass followed me into the house. I was just reaching for the box of dog biscuits to reward her when Maggie swooped into the kitchen, growled, and began dragging Lass away from me by the ruff of her neck. Because the attack was a complete surprise and the floor was slick, Lass was hauled all the way to the step leading up to the living room before she was able to twist free. Swiftly Maggie presented herself to me for a biscuit.

"Why, you jealous little snip, you certainly didn't earn a biscuit with that performance. What got into you anyway? Were you mad because I spent a little time with Lass?"

But that didn't seem logical. If Maggie were an affectionate dog, if there were strong ties between her and me, then some sign of jealousy toward a new dog would have been expected. But Maggie was so independent, so unneedful of my attention, that I couldn't credit her action to envy.

For the next week, until the first snow fell, Lass and I worked with the sheep for a short time every morning, and each time we came in from the orchard Maggie repeated her assaults, dragging Lass as far away from me as she could. Finally I concluded that Maggie just didn't like the smell of sheep.

4

With the coming of the first snow, herding sessions were abandoned for the winter. Lass had been bred to the sire of the first Megan, and although she had not yet begun to thicken, I didn't want her around the sheep. One of the Marys had developed a habit of turning to butt at Lass when the dog tried to herd her, and I was afraid of injury to Lass and the unborn pups.

Christmas holidays came, bringing an unusual number of guests to Touchwood. The dogs' individualities were becoming more apparent now, and they showed most clearly at the arrival of company. Lass, whom I had at first believed to be a thoroughly friendly dog, was suspicious of strangers. She stood close beside me as I let them in, sometimes growling softly. When I said, "It's okay, Lass; he's an uncle not a burglar," she would come forward, wagging, but her legs remained stiff and quickly came back to my side. She never offered to snap, and she was unfailingly loving with children, but she seemed to feel that unfamiliar adults were suspect.

Maggie, who was, toward me, the least affectionate of all the dogs, met every stranger with delight and open, unquestioning welcome. With the coming of winter Roy had begun stopping by occasionally in the evenings to tussle with the dogs and to sit quietly while I played "When You And I Were Young," on the piano. He always brought dog biscuits, and this probably had something to do with the intensity of Maggie's greetings. Still it seemed odd to me that the little fox flung herself so hungrily at anyone who came to the door, but hung back, always, at my return to the house when the other dogs swamped me with welcome.

Lad, at four months, wavered between following Maggie's example and Lass's when the doorbell rang, but his natural inclinations were obvious. He was a lover, like Riff.

One evening after the holidays were past it occurred to me that Lad was old enough to learn a simple command or two. Lass was asleep on the kitchen floor; the living room was too warm for her when there was a fire in the fireplace. Riff was outdoors barking at his squirrel, and Maggie was curled up on one of the windowseats that flanked the fireplace. Lad, who was quietly mouthing his favorite possession, a cow's jawbone with teeth intact, seemed neither too boisterous nor too sleepy for a lesson.

I called him to me, laid the monstrous bone on top of

the piano where he couldn't see it, and said, "Laddie, sit."

I had just bent over to push him into sitting position when suddenly Maggie was there. She crowded in between Lad and me, and sat. Sitting would seem to be a passive thing, but Maggie sat so tightly, so tense and eager and close to my feet, that she conveyed an impression of vibrant action. Her bright little face was pointed straight up toward mine. Her eyes glowed.

"Okay, Magpie, that was a good sit," I said softly. "Now you have to stay up here out of the way so Lad can have a chance." I scooped her up and planted her on the windowseat with the repeated command to stay.

She stayed, but it seemed to me that at every "sit" command I gave Lad, Maggie tightened herself into such a concentration of sittingness that her size decreased by half.

After that, for short periods in the evenings, I began working with all the dogs except Riff, for whom any kind of command brought forth waves of blank-minded apology. Maggie's lessons were just reviews of last fall's obedience training, but she reveled in the chance to perform. Lad and Lass learned a few simple commands and enjoyed the lessons as much as Maggie.

Ordinarily all dogs except the immediate pupil were shut out of the room during a lesson, but one night I let Maggie stay while I worked with Lass. Maggie was ordered to stay on the windowseat, as a test of her steadiness to the "stay" command.

Lass and I had been working on "come." Although she knew what to do, she did not yet know that she *must* do it, and do it directly, with no rug-sniffing along the way. Until tonight we had been working with a long cord attached to her collar so that I could reel her in if she didn't come immediately. She had become perfect as long as the rope was on, but now it was time to test her without it.

I sat her at the north end of the room and went to the south end. "Lass, come!"

She came like an arrow.

"Good old girl. You're wonderful."

Maggie sat motionless, her eyes darting from me to Lass, and back to me.

We repeated the "come" command again and again. On the fourth time Lass held back, testing me.

I opened my mouth to repeat the command, but before I could, Maggie had flashed between us. Growling nastily, she sank her teeth into Lass's throat. With her short legs braced into the carpet she hauled Lass across the room in a straight line to my feet. When they arrived, Maggie was jubilant, Lass was dumbfounded, and I was laughing out of control.

I picked Maggie up and cuddled her. "Mag, my love, I appreciate your help, but when I need a teaching assistant, I'll let you know, okay? Now butt out."

Except for her training periods Maggie's petulant behavior continued. Several times a day she sat outside the dog door striking it with her paw. Bang-bang-bang-bang-bang. If I ignored her, the banging became louder and angrier. Usually she started the racket when I was deeply concentrating on my work, or during a television comedian's punch line. Eventually I always gave in and went to open the kitchen door for her. She would rise, grin, wag, and stroll inside, satisfied.

With the onset of serious winter weather Lass was allowed to stay in the house at night. Maggie had recently given up her bed in the cold woodshed and had begun sleeping on the foot of my bed. She did not curl up against my feet as Riff did, at least not at the beginning of the night, but by morning she was always stretched out against my legs. It was a tentative gesture, and as soon as she knew I was awake, she jumped down.

The first night Lass stayed indoors, she settled down on the floor close beside the bed. Maggie's ears went flat against her head. Stiffly she jumped down from the bed and, head low, eyes baleful, stalked out of the room, through the house, and out the dog door. I waited an hour or so, then went to the kitchen, mumbling and fumbling for light switches as I went. In the snow-reflected moonlight of the shed I saw the heart-shaped white spot pointed at me. She was lying in the coldest, draftiest corner of the cold, drafty shed, on bare concrete.

"Come on in, Maggie. We love you."

She did not move.

"Please, Maggie, come in where it's warm. My feet will get cold if you don't, and so will yours."

Her only answer was to lower her head and close her eyes.

I gave up and went back to bed, expecting at any moment to hear the dog door start banging. It didn't. The next morning she was still curled miserably on the shed floor.

More and more frequently during January Maggie's petulance curdled into vandalism. Feeling dull and heavy with winter confinement, I began walking the length of the lane every morning to get the mail, taking a different dog with me each day. On the first day I took Maggie, and then Lad and Riff. On the fourth day I took Lass.

When we got home, both of the pillows on the davenport had been disemboweled. Bits of corduroy and foam rubber were scattered everywhere, even through the kitchen and den.

Maggie was in the woodshed, curled up and shivering.

As I began the chore of picking billions of flakes of shredded foam rubber out of the deep shaggy carpet, I grew more and more angry. It would be pointless to punish her now. She wouldn't know why she was being punished, and would simply be confused and resentful. All of my dogs, from early puppyhood, had been purposely accustomed to being left in the house alone. None of them had ever been destructive, except for Riff's vengeful urinating.

When I had done what I could with the living room, I placed a phone call to the classified ad department of a dog magazine and dictated an ad to be run the following month, offering for sale a young obedience-trained border collie bitch.

5

Megan was seldom in my conscious thoughts now even though there were occasional recurrences of the dream that had begun after she was killed, a dream in which I knew she had been merely stunned, not killed, and had been buried alive. I was striving frantically to find the place where she was buried before it was too late.

Still, in my eagerness for the birth of Lass's pups there was an element of hope for another Megan. The sire of the litter was Megan's sire, and Lass greatly resembled Megan's dam. Then, too, this litter marked my beginning as a serious breeder of dogs.

In Riff's youth he and his mate Molly had produced several good litters of Bedlington terriers, but somehow this was different. I was settled at Touchwood now, with a genuine kennel building, genuine runs, and all the paraphernalia of the dog fancy, the accumulation of which had been such fun.

As a child I had squatted for long hours behind the greeting-card rack in the drugstore, absorbing the pages and pictures in dog magazines. I sang the wonderful names beneath the photographs—Champion Parader's Bold Venture, Champion Rock Ridge

Night Rocket. I peered nearsightedly into the tiny photographs, memorizing every line of the dogs and of the backgrounds, and I imagined what my kennel was going to be like, what magnificent names I would give my dogs.

As a very young woman I had worked in other people's kennels, chafing under practices I disagreed with and planning how I was going to run *my* kennel someday.

In reality Touchwood Kennel was just a tiny hip-roofed chicken house, patched with wood from a disassembled outhouse, scrubbed and disinfected and painted bright red with white windows and door. It had only three fenced runs, and it sat in the orchard where in wintertime the winds struck it without relief. But it was a beginning.

As Lass's delivery grew near, I sat for long quiet stretches of time with my hand on her upturned abdomen, rejoicing in the stirring mass of pups under my palm. I waited, and Lass waited. She wanted always to be against me now. When I sat down to eat, she jammed her head across my lap and held it there throughout the meal. When I tried to play the piano, she thrust her head under my arm and knocked my hand up off the keys. She was uneasy and insatiable in her demands for assurance.

Maggie spent more and more time in the woodshed or galloping over the wind-formed ridges of snow in the dog yard. Often I looked out the kitchen windows to see her curled in the snow at the base of the huge old maple trees, napping or pretending to while the wind parted her coat and drove ice at her skin. Sometimes when I went outdoors and coaxed, she would come in, but as soon as Lass won my attention away from her, the little dog went outdoors again. I shivered to see her lying out there, but my sympathy was lessened by the knowledge that it was her own silly decision.

On a Tuesday morning in early February the pups began to arrive. I shut out the other dogs, who were curious about the odor of birth, and sat with Lass on the pantry floor. It was a large light pantry in the heart of the house, and directly beneath its floor was the mammoth old-fashioned furnace, so the floor was always pleasantly warm to the touch. In the intermission between the arrival of the first and second pups, I made a cup of tea and brought it into the pantry, then forgot to drink it in the excitement of the arrivals.

Lass was calm after the first birth. She showed no pain or anxiety, just a fervent sort of mastery of the situation. I refrained from handling each pup until her attention was on the next born; then I picked up the last, examined it, whispered, "Male" or "Female" or "You've got too much white on you, honey, but we love you anyway."

After the fifth I began to relax. Five was all I'd hoped for, and so far there were three females.

"I hope one of you is Mairi," I murmured. That was the name I had selected for the one female I planned to keep, providing there was one who met my standards of brightness, affection, attractive markings, and over-all quality.

By noon a sixth pup appeared and, at increasingly long intervals through the afternoon, a seventh, eighth, and ninth. Lass was weary and empty; I was jubilant.

Maggie was outside banging the dog door.

For the next few days my attention was never long away from Lass and the pups. The typewriter re-mained covered; dishes gathered in the sink. I sat on the pantry floor, unaware of the passing of time, memorizing each pup and trying on names.

Lad and Riff didn't seem to mind my absence particularly. They romped in the snow or played quiet tug-of-war games in the living room. Maggie stayed outdoors for long periods of time, but when driven inside by the sub-zero cold, she sat across the kitchen from the pantry door, her head cocked slightly, her penetrating eyes moving from Lass to the pups to me. When I poured loving praise on Lass, Maggie's head cocked a notch farther.

In all the nine pups there was, surprisingly, no runt. They were nearly equal in size and vitality, and they all thrived. I studied most carefully the four females. One was unattractively marked and had a slightly shorter head than the others, but any one of the other three, at this stage, appeared to be a potential Mairi.

"Lassie, lady dog, you did a wonderful job," I murmured over and over while Lass stretched herself in the luxury of the praise.

Maggie listened and watched.

On the morning of the third day I slept much later than usual and woke to find the world beyond the windows swept away in a shifting cloud of white. If the sun had risen, it was invisible behind the wind-driven snow. By noon the snow had ceased to fall, but the wind roared around the house, moving the new snow in the thirty-foot billows across the cornfields. The temperature dropped to zero, then below. Even Maggie preferred the living room to the outdoors. I went out just once, to feed the sheep and to be sure the car's engine warmer was plugged in; then I came back through the woodshed, piled my arms with enough apple wood to last all afternoon and evening, and prepared for a long winter's night.

The wind had done something to the television antenna so I decided this would be a good time to appease my annual New Year's self-improvement resolution. I put on some quiet records, picked up a volume of Emerson's essays, and settled into the big chair closest to the fire. Supper was a plate of Christmas gift cheeses and a mug of tomato soup that warmed my fingers and my stomach.

About nine the phone rang. It was Roy's son, a middle-aged man who farmed a few miles north of town. I had met him briefly last summer.

"We took Dad to the hospital yesterday," he said. "He's going to be all right, but he had a slight heart attack yesterday morning, out shoveling snow."

Oh no, I thought.

The man went on. "I hate to ask this, but in all the excitement nobody fed Star. Yesterday or today. I was wondering if you would be able to get over there maybe tomorrow and throw a little hay down for her. I'd come over and do it myself, but with this new snow today our darn road out here is drifted shut and I don't know when the plows will be able to get out."

I assured him that I'd be happy to take care of Star for as long as necessary. After I hung up, I went to the front windows to look across the field at the indistinct black shape of Star's barn, some two blocks away. The wind had died down, and the moon was high and full, sending a pale blue glow up from the white earth.

"Should I go over and feed her now, or wait till morning?" I asked the dogs who milled around me. "Oh, heck, might as well go now. It won't be too bad out, with the wind turned off, and for all I know it might be worse tomorrow. Besides, poor old Star must be getting pretty hungry, especially in her delicate condition."

As I began working into the requisite layers of boots, hooded sweat shirt, insulated coveralls, jacket, scarf, and gloves, I reflected on how little one appreciates, in summer, the luxury of being able merely to open a door and walk outside. By the time I was booted, buttoned, zipped, and mittened, I felt rather like a giant asthmatic toddler.

I looked down at the dogs, all of whom stood watching tensely to see if the word would be, "Yes, you can go," or "Sorry, gang." Their eyes were glued on mine, and Lad was already edging toward the front door in order to be the first one out.

One dog would be nice for company, I decided. In the back of my mind were vague and improbable visions born of television Lassies, visions in which I lay freezing in the cornfield with a broken leg while my anthropomorphic dog went to call an ambulance. Not Lad or Riff, I decided. Too silly. And not Maggie. She had a dangerous habit of nipping at Star's heels and inviting a hoof-cracked skull.

Lass was the obvious choice. She waited tensely for my signal. For the past three days she had hardly been out of the house, and I realized that she would probably love to stretch her legs. When I looked in at the pups, they were lying in a motionless heap, their stomachs stretched with milk. They wouldn't be needing Lass for a while.

Lass and I started out across the cornfield. Snow lay in the lane in ranges of drifts as high as my head, but the field itself, which was slightly higher, was blown nearly clear. However, the five or six inches of snow that remained in the field was crusted, not enough to bear weight but just enough to break with every step and make walking tiresome work. I was moving diagonally across the field, so that the ridges and valleys of the corn rows passed at an angle beneath my feet, adding to the difficulty of finding sure footing. But the field was bright with lunar glow, and the cold was not yet uncomfortable.

I said to Lass, " 'The moon, on the breast of the new fallen snow, gave the luster of midday to objects below.' " She circled back, wagged, and dashed off again in a skidding orgy of freedom.

It would have been an enjoyable moonlight hike except for its cause. Roy in the hospital. Heart attack. Even a minor one must have been a frightening experience for him, I thought. Or perhaps more frustrating than frightening, considering the temperament of the man. He must be chafing at the hospital rules, eager to get back to his own house, to Star, to the chess set he was making in his workshop for a niece.

I wondered what it had felt like to him when he knew something was happening to his heart, whether he had lain on the sidewalk for a long time, who had found him and taken him to the hospital. Illogically I felt guilty, as though I should have kept closer track of him, made sure he was all right. I thought about the times he had called Touchwood to be sure I wasn't ill or injured just because he hadn't seen me for a few days.

My leg muscles ached by the time Lass and I reached the barn, and the skin of my face was stiff with cold.

It was a small red barn, just three large box stalls opening onto the paddock, with a tack room and woodworking shop added at one end. Star was inside her stall. She whickered and rustled around to face me.

"Did you think we were going to let you starve to death?"

I cupped my hand over her muzzle, then moved back along her side and felt her drum-tight abdomen where the foal was growing. The curve seemed more distinct than it had last week. I pulled off my glove to feel the warm hard skin, the bulging veins, and beneath them the lumps that might be the foal's head or knee or hip. Pleasure shivered up my spine.

I realized suddenly that I should have brought a flashlight. The barn was familiar to me, but I had no idea where the light switches were, or even if there were any. And now that I was here I realized also that I didn't know where the oats were kept or how to get up to the haymow.

By much groping and fumbling, the feeding and watering were eventually accomplished, but I was not entirely sure that it was hay and not straw I'd put in the manger, or that I had indeed hit the grain box when I poured the measure of oats. I was thoroughly cold by this time, and imbedded deep in the heel of my right hand was a large splinter. I decided to revive myself in Roy's house before facing the Arctic wasteland between here and home.

The house was unlocked, as houses customarily were here. Lass followed me inside. I felt uneasy, stealthy, being in the house, but I also felt warm. I turned on the kitchen light, pried off my boots, and stood for long luscious moments while the hot grill of the register burned into my feet through two layers of wool socks.

The teakettle was on the stove. On the counter by the bread box was the jar of instant tea Roy kept for my visits. Feeling less and less like a housebreaker, I turned on one burner and filled the kettle.

Suddenly there was a harsh knock at the front door. Lass growled and lifted her hackles. For a second I stood shaken by the guilty pounding of my heart; then, as I went toward the door, I saw the flashing red light of the town's one police car.

"Its okay, Jack. It's only me," I called as I opened the front door. "I'm not burgling."

His face relaxed and he smiled. "Just thought I'd better check when I saw the light," he said. "I knew Roy wouldn't be out of the hospital yet."

"Come on in and have a cup of tea with me. I was down feeding Star and got cold. How is Roy—have you heard?"

He reckoned he'd better not leave his car radio, but we visited at the door until the whistling kettle called me back to the kitchen.

Half an hour later, thawed, recharged, and freed of the splinter, I went back out into the cold and set my course across the field toward the lights that shone around Touchwood's front door. Lass stayed closer to me on the return trip. The temperature was dropping and the wind rising again. Before we had fairly started, my fingertips had disappeared in pain and my forehead was brittle against the wind. With every step I advanced, Touchwood seemed to retreat.

But gradually we gained on it, and my fingerless hand was turning the doorknob. Lad and Riff hit us with a wall of welcome. Lass went to check on her pups while I poked up the glowing log in the fireplace and began to fight my way out of boots, coveralls, scarf, sweat shirt. Glasses steamed, and cold crept painfully out of fingertips and toes.

I turned on the radio, hoping to catch the half-hour weather report so that I'd know whether to go down to the basement and plug in the auxiliary heater which, on nights colder than twenty below, kept the kitchen water pipes from freezing. But while the weatherman was still involved in the irrelevancies of high-pressure fronts in Canada, Lass came to me and stood whining. It was the first time I had ever heard her whine.

Suddenly fearful that something might be wrong with the pups, I left the periphery of the fire and went to the pantry. Lass followed close against my knee, still whining.

Before the pups' birth I had replaced the old solid pantry door with a screen door so the warmth from the kitchen could get into the pantry. The screen door was hooked, as I had left it, but the bottom panel of screen had been pushed inward.

I turned on the light. Three small black pups swam blindly in place in the center of the newspapered floor.

Only three.

"Well, Lass, where are the rest of them?" I asked in a

soft, puzzled voice. I searched carefully behind
brooms and dust mops and vacuum cleaner, around
and beneath all the dog-food sacks and grocers' cartons
that accumulated in the pantry, while my mind evaded
the meaning of the torn screen.

The missing pups were not in the pantry, and I had
known they would not be. I ran to the woodshed door
and, with trembling hands, turned the doorknob. The
light bulb in the shed had burned out, but my flashlight showed what I feared to see.

Maggie lay on her side in her wind-chilled corner of
the shed, her head up and cocked. Her eyes were
bright at the sight of me, and her tail struck the cold
concrete. The expression on her small face was unmis-
takably proud, expectant. She held herself in readiness
for the praise she had watched me pour on Lass when
her pups were born.

Along Maggie's side lay the six pups. They did not
move.

Three hours later I got into bed, but, still too agitated
to lie down, I sat in a cross-legged hunch under a cape
of quilts, and stared out the window at the pines and
the field beyond.

Lad and Riff were long since asleep in the living
room. Lass was in the pantry with her three remaining
pups. I didn't know where Maggie was, and I didn't
care.

The two stolen pups that had not quite been dead

when I found them had been put through every chill-fighting technique I knew, and had finally died in my hands. All the female pups were gone, all the potential Mairis.

I was finished with the tears of loss and frustration, but I felt old and heavy, sitting there looking out of the big black house. I wanted to pick up the phone and call someone, to tell some sympathetic friend what had happened. But no one among my acquaintances would have welcomed such a call, or any call, at one-thirty in the morning.

Suddenly Maggie appeared at the edge of the bed. In the darkness only her white forehead heart showed. She hesitated, asking permission.

"Yes, come on up. I'm not mad at you," I said wearily.

She sprang, and came to sit tightly in front of me. Automatically my hands began ironing down the curls over her ribs. She was trembling.

My attention came in from the pine trees then and focused on her. Her trembling came in spasms, shaking her briefly, then smoothing out for a second or two. Her round red-brown eyes were fixed on mine. Her head was up, but her body, legs, and tail seemed drawn up smaller than life.

"Maggie, *why* did you have to do it?" I whispered.

But I knew why. The knowledge had been with me as long as Maggie herself. From the first she had received a smaller measure of love than Riff and her predecessor and, later, Lad and Lass. It had not been intentional. The others had simply been easier dogs to love.

I cupped her face in my hands and smoothed back her ears, drawing her eyes into Oriental slits. Her trembling quieted, and she moved a fraction of an inch closer to me.

"But you always seemed so independent, as though you didn't care whether I noticed you or not."

I talked to her silently, thinking the words and transmitting them through my eyes and hers. Somehow I didn't want my voice to bring the other dogs just now.

"You never wanted to be petted or held like the rest of them," I reasoned. "You were always tearing off somewhere, hiding in the corn or sulking in the shed. Was that part of it? Were you trying to get my attention then, and when you banged the door and tore things up and picked on the other dogs? And when you took Lassie's babies?"

The words sent my memory veering off toward a little girl, a silent, belligerently lonely child with an older sister who was beautiful and a younger sister who was good; a child who stole money from her Sunday School envelopes in a blind longing to be recognized, to buy love.

Maggie and I were perhaps not so far apart.

I lay down, and for the first time, Maggie curled up against me and slept.

6

After that night a subtle but strengthening rapport began to grow between Maggie and me. With an odd sort of feeling of atonement, I started making a conscious effort to single her out for attention, and with perhaps a similar feeling of atonement, she responded. For the next few days she circled the pantry door widely and guiltily, flattening her ears and looking in my direction as though expecting blows. But gradually she forgot the debacle of the pups, and so did I, nearly.

When I came into the house now, it was Maggie I reached for first, greeting the other dogs in passing but concentrating my welcome on the small fox-faced dog at the outer edge of the crowd. At first she hung back and had to be coaxed, but before long she was the first to fling herself at me with all the gusto she had formerly reserved for Roy and strangers.

When I settled into the corner of the davenport with a book or a manuscript, it was Maggie I invited up beside me. The other dogs crowded in, too, but theirs were stabler egos, and if I held them aside in favor of Maggie, they were only briefly disappointed.

I expected some response on Maggie's part, but I was not prepared for the opening up that came. It was tentative at first, as though she were suspicious of the attention in which she basked. But as the days and weeks passed, Maggie bloomed in her newfound sunshine. Gradually she ceased banging the dog door. If I began to play with one of the other dogs, she no longer snarled and hauled the interloper away by the scruff of the neck. Instead she moved to whatever part of me she could get to, and allowed the other dog to share me with her.

When answers to the dog magazine ad began coming in, I explained, with some embarrassment, that I had decided not to sell the dog after all.

In the spring we resumed our training sessions. If Maggie had been a quick pupil before, she was even quicker now that her tensions were erased. She performed with the same smooth eagerness that the first Megan had shown.

One night in May there was a knock at the door. I had fallen asleep on the davenport after a full day of painting the orchard fence, and I sat up, startled and disoriented by sleep and the sudden knock. The ten-o'clock news was just beginning on television. People in our town didn't drop in on one another at ten o'clock at night.

I hurried to the door in a cloud of dogs. It was Roy.

"Come on in," I said, trying to clear a path to the living room through the dogs. The old man's face was strangely unsmiling.

We sat down on the davenport with the delighted Maggie between us. Having received their welcoming pats, the other dogs went back to their napping, Riff and Lass on the windowseats and Lad in his current favorite spot under the piano with his head across the pedals.

"What's wrong?" I asked.

Roy sighed, a ragged sound. "Well, sis, we don't have our Star anymore."

The foal had been due any time; in fact I had called Roy's house twice that day, but he hadn't answered the phone.

He went on. "The colt was born the middle of last night, and I thought everything was okay, but I guess Star had a twisted gut. The vet and me, we worked on her all day. She died just a little bit ago."

"Oh, no, Roy." Not Star, I thought. Any other horse but her.

"I think the colt's going to make it all right, though," he said. "It's a nice little bay filly, and she's sound and strong. I've bottle-fed worse-looking ones than this before, and had 'em live."

But I wasn't listening. I was remembering the cadence of the little mare's singlefoot gait, her fast walk and slow rocking canter. I was seeing the lane, the baseball diamond, the woods, and the mill valley framed between her small stiff ears.

I began to cry.

At the sound, Maggie suddenly braced herself with her back to me, lowered her head, raised her hackles, and growled a softly serious warning at the old gentleman who was her first love.

So surprising was her action that I stopped crying and stared at her. Swiftly Maggie twisted around to lick the tears from my face. Then, pressed close against my side, she resumed her defiance of Roy.

I understood suddenly.

Maggie sensed that I was unhappy and that Roy was somehow hurting me, causing my unhappiness. She was puzzled, because Roy was a friend, and yet her small body was braced in my defense.

I glanced at the other dogs. Lad was snoring softly under the piano; Riff was asleep; Lass lay awake and uneasily watchful on the windowseat, but only Maggie had grasped the situation and acted on it. The fact that her understanding was faulty made the gesture no less fine.

"It's all right, Mag." I pulled her into my arms, laughter rising through the crying-hiccups. To the amazed Roy I explained, "She thinks you're hurting me."

With my voice back to normal, Maggie relaxed, twisted again to lick my face, then offered to Roy her apologetically lowered head. His knobbed hand smoothed over the heart on her forehead.

I made a pot of tea then, and we settled down to talk about what a good little mare Star had been, and what we might name the new filly. Then, as he often did, Roy began to reminisce about horses he had had as a boy and the ponies his children and grandchildren grew up with. His face was light and happy with the pleasure of his memories.

Because I knew the stories by heart and could listen with only a small part of my attention, I curled into a more comfortable position in my corner of the davenport and let my mind and my hands rest on Maggie. Slowly my palms smoothed down the curly places over her shoulders.

I thought about her extraordinary sensitivity, which I had failed to recognize and, in so failing, had injured countless times with slights that would not have been felt by most dogs.

I thought about that once-in-a-lifetime dog that I had assumed was lost with the loss of Megan.

And I smiled.

About the Author

For several years Lynn Hall has devoted herself full-time to writing books for young readers. This is her eighth book for Follett.

Miss Hall was born in a suburb of Chicago and was raised in Des Moines, Iowa. She has always loved dogs and horses and has kept them around her whenever possible. As a child, she was limited to stray dogs, neighbors' horses, and the animals found in library books. But as an adult, she has owned and shown several horses and has worked with dogs, both as a veterinarian's assistant and a handler on the dog show circuit. Many of her books are about dogs and horses.

Miss Hall lives in a one-hundred-year-old farm-house near the village of Garnavillo, Iowa. Besides writing, she works as coordinator and counselor for a local telephone counseling service offering help to troubled young people. Her leisure-time is spent reading, playing the piano, or exploring the nearby hills and woodlands on horseback or foot, with a dog or two at her heels.